Lessons from the Borderlands

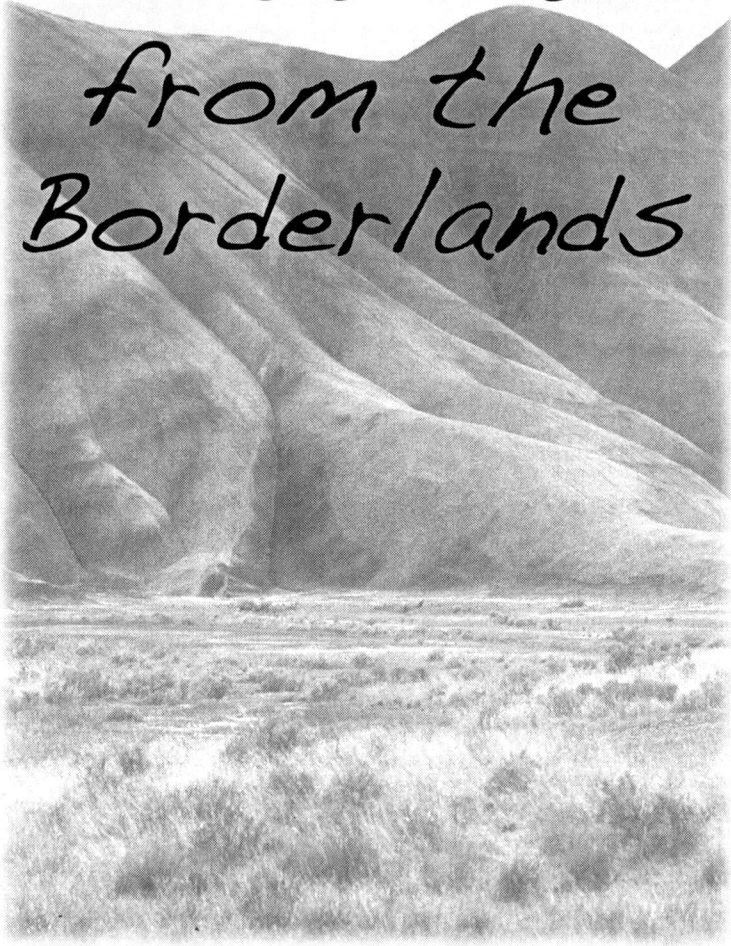

Bette Lynch Husted

Plain View Press
http://plainviewpress.net

3800 N. Lamar, Suite 730-260
Austin, TX 78756

ISBN: 978-1-935514-85-5
Library of Congress Control Number: 2011945372

Cover art: © Gregory Johnston Dreamstime.com
Cover design by Sherry L. Pilisko

Acknowledgements
    I would like to thank the editors of the journals in which earlier versions of these essays first appeared: "Art Appreciation" in *Oregon Humanities: A Journal of Ideas and Perspectives*, Spring 2002; "Body Mechanics" in *Fourth Genre* Issue 4.2, Fall 2002; "Hope, for the Dry Side" in *College English*, Volume 64, Number 2, November 2001; "Jointly" in *Under the Sun*, Volume XI, Number 1, Summer 2006; "Personal Hygiene" in *Prairie Schooner*, Volume 80, Number 3, Fall 2006; "Looking for Soapstone" in *Silk Road*, Volume 2, Number 1, Spring 2007; "A Place to Sleep" in *Oregon Humanities*, Fall/Winter 2007; a portion of "Considering the Possibilities" in *"Quality and Equality: the Journey Ahead," Teaching English in the Two Year College Special Issue:* 25th Anniversary, Volume 27, Number 1, September 1999.
    I am grateful to the Oregon Arts Commission for a 2007 Individual Artist Fellowship, and for residencies at Soapstone's Writing Retreat for Women and the Fishtrap Imnaha cabin, where some of these essays were written.
    I am deeply grateful for the teachers who brought me stories—especially my mother, and for students, who have also been my teachers. Eugenie Fyfe has been a lifelong guide. My thanks to Judith Barrington and Caroline Le Guin, who offered early readings of these essays, and to Molly Gloss, whose vision helped me see their final shape more clearly. Special thanks to Jeannette Cappella for her wisdom and support throughout the writing of this book, and for helping me believe our stories can be heard.
    Always, in all ways, thanks to Dean.

For Emily, Irene, and Carolyn
and for Jeannette

"The truth is, I am trying to change things," says Bette Lynch Husted. Yet throughout these essays there is no polemical ranting; rather there are small stones set like prayer beads upon the page. These polished stones, the words themselves, examine through a gentle and reasoned voice, a teacher's voice, the kind of teacher we have all wanted, one who listened as she opened up new a vision on a known, or accepted, world.

These stories have components of myth: personal journey, history, and hope. "Who have we been? Who do we want to be? Why are we here? How should we live? Do the people who find their way through the world without wading down creek beds simply know the right stories? The ones that will keep them from getting lost?" Husted asks. But her stories are not myth. They convey what it is like to still feel less than, other, apart, not deserving—and how hearing such labels used, and misused, can give us "the feeling that my real self was all wrong" and even limit ourselves. In these essays such limits are not confined to just race, or gender; they include the great unspoken (not spoken of) class divisions.

But again we are offered possibilities, more stones to carry; we can listen to one another, we can offer each other stories and truths, about our lives, what we need, what we want. We need to be quiet. We need to listen. *Lessons from the Borderlands* gives us tools to begin.

M.E. Hope, author of *The Past is Clean*

Contents

The Blue Sky Story

I'm with friends, writers who have spent the week together at the Oregon coast, a full carload of laughing women on their way out to dinner. We've had a great time. But as the highway winds its way up Neahkanie Mountain and cuts across the cliff face high above the Pacific, I can't stop thinking about something that happened this morning. "Let's write for twenty minutes," Jan had suggested. "Here's a topic: we." The others sat for a moment, considering the possibilities, but I had already started: *In spite of our years of practice, those of us who grow up poor remain unsure. We speak the same language as everyone else, but it feels as if we don't know all the words.*

"You know," Franny would muse when we shared what we had written, "I've heard other people say this, too. But it's never quite made sense to me. Doesn't everything change once someone goes off to college? You even became a college teacher yourself, Bette..."

It was the question I've spent my life trying to answer, yet I didn't know what to say.

The sun is hanging just above the ocean's rim now, a red half-disk floating on its own mysteries. We pile out of the car and Brooke holds open the heavy door of the Blue Sky Restaurant, grinning at each of us as we pass. It's a celebration, a party. No one is ready for our week to end.

The young woman who greets us can't find our names on the reservation list. She knows we can see an empty table just over her left shoulder—bathed in summer-evening light, white napkins folded into coronets, glasses with tall stems—but another party will be coming in an hour, she says, and at the Blue Sky a meal is an experience, not something we should hurry through. Franny turns to us, her face flushed. I picture the fish and chips place we passed a few miles back, all of us wiping greasy fingers on paper napkins and laughing, but I don't say anything, and the others are as adamant as Franny. No, we don't want to look for another restaurant. Finally the woman escorts us to the table. She's sorry about the time crunch, she says. Now she is smiling. "And this is Aaron, who will serve you tonight."

By the time we have ordered wine and finished the appetizer and asked for a second one, an amazing creation of tiny delectables to wrap in grape leaves, most of our hour has ticked away, but no one else seems to have noticed. I have decided on the salmon, so when Aaron tells me that tonight's specialty is also a salmon dish, I say yes. The special is something they can serve quickly. The light has dimmed and by our table's candle I can barely make out what's on my plate when the food arrives. It's the same salmon the people who have lived along the Columbia River for centuries skewer on willow sticks that lean toward the fire's glowing coals, I tell myself—the kind they'll be honoring at the longhouse on the next Salmon Feast. The fish I see on license plates on every road in Oregon. It has a slightly different flavor, but it's very good.

Then my fork finds a mouthful of salmon touched by the dark sauce spreading over one end of the fish and onto whatever is next to it on the plate, a mysterious heap of rice or vegetables I can't quite make out in the dimness, and something burns a cindery hole down toward my heart. My God. It's the hottest thing I have ever tasted. I reach for my glass, a small, delicate thing holding perhaps a half-cup of water. My throat has nearly closed. Will I be able to breathe? The water dissolves against the roof of my mouth.

But I am still alive. No one has noticed my panic. I look at Brooke's water glass. Should I? No. No. Shallow breaths; no, deep. Nothing works. Another black-and-white waiter with a water pitcher weaves through the tables, and I catch his eye. Again he comes, and again. Jan is telling a story that makes everyone laugh, then listen earnestly. I am not going to die. The pain has subsided, I tell myself, because I am bearing it. It must have become bearable.

"This is so good," says Brooke. Jan's halibut is wonderful, too. The young waiter returns, filling my glass for a fourth time. "I can tell who had the special tonight," he laughs. "They're the ones wanting all these refills!"

"May I have a bite of the salmon?" Franny asks. Sure, I say, but be careful. It's very hot on this end. Franny takes a bite, then leaps up—napkin to her mouth, her fork clattering onto her plate. She runs for the restroom.

"I wondered why you changed your order from the regular salmon to this," Jan will say as the story unfolds. "But I thought you knew what you were doing." I roll my eyes; everyone laughs. Habanera peppers, Brooke explains. The hottest known variety.

No, someone will correct me later, offering as evidence a list of the twenty-five hottest peppers: habaneras are second. Not really inferior, just not quite as desirable.

⊱─◆─○─◆─⊰

The next day, on the long drive back up the Columbia River Gorge toward rural eastern Oregon and the small town where I live, I had plenty of time to think about what had happened. Franny was right: I have been to college. And I have spent my life as a teacher—trying hard to hold those magical doors open for others, not simply so they could escape the hard physical work that broke my father's body, but so they could see and feel and understand more of what it means to be a human being, have access to more ideas and tools of discovery and means of creating beauty. "You are curious, creative, courageous," I have told student after student, class after class. "Look what you have done; imagine what you'll do next!" Why, then, hadn't I dropped my fork and run, too, or at least let the others know I was in trouble? It wasn't cowardice, some simple weak-kneed shyness—teachers are performers, acrobats always on stage—and I couldn't imagine any student of mine saying I hesitated to voice my convictions. Yet something about those moments in the Blue Sky Restaurant felt all too familiar.

Years before, wearing my last clean pair of worn Levis, I had left my husband holding our still-in-diapers son in a steamy laundromat while I looked for fabric in the store across the street. A Master's degree in English and my high school teaching job had allowed us to buy our first home together, a used trailer, but the previous occupants had taken the drapes with them and I would have to make curtains. Then we could begin to look for a second-hand washing machine that would fit in the tiny walk-through bathroom. For a while, at least, we'd have to hang diapers on the clothesline. I was fingering a bolt of beige fabric—is this heavy enough?—when a clerk spoke at my elbow. "Are your hands clean?"

"What did you say?" Dean asked me when he saw my face. "Nothing," I told him. I took the baby back and held him close. "I couldn't remember words."

A pair of turkey vultures launched themselves from the basalt cliffs and wheeled out over the river, riding the currents of the sky. Don't know the right words, can't remember words: at some deep level I already knew, had known even last night, the source of my silence. What had happened at the Blue Sky was about class, or rather the lingering lessons of my childhood's social class. That sudden, stunned feeling that I don't belong.

Of course, I thought, not everyone who grew up in a working class family would have reacted to those peppers the way I did. Some people seem comfortable anywhere, at ease whether or not they know the codes of conduct. And some—most, I supposed—have memorized enough words and phrases to line them up in order almost every time. Hide under a different kind of silence. Still, isn't everyone affected by the lessons of class, whether we are unconsciously following their rules, their patterns of seeing the world, or consciously trying to learn new patterns? Franny's bold reaction to that hot-pepper sauce had been as instinctive as my silence. Add to class the lessons of our individual experiences with race—or rather, "whiteness," the idea that one group is inherently more blessed, more worthy of success than another—and gender. The messages we heard on the playground about our physical abilities or lack of them, and later about our mental and emotional health. Our sexual orientation. We assume we're sharing the same cultural reality, that our reality is everyone else's, more or less: eating, sleeping, taking a bath, getting dressed. But each of us has learned our own life's lessons, so each of us filters even these mundane activities through a different lens. No wonder we struggle to understand each other.

At the freeway rest stop, I found myself looking into the faces of my fellow travelers, wondering. Two brown-skinned boys raced each other across the parking lot, nearly colliding with the white-haired women—sisters, I imagined—who were balancing elbow to elbow, each holding the other up. A woman leaned into her car to buckle her child into a car seat. A man lifted his gray-muzzled black Lab out of his van and set him gently on the narrow strip of grass. What had happened in these people's lives? How did they see the world? If we met over a cup of coffee—or milkshakes, in the case of those boys—could we listen to each other?

Stories about race and gender are hard to share, even when we try. Class, though, is the area we simply won't talk about. It's not just difficult, it's inappropriate. Affluent and even middle class people might think it unnecessary, preposterous, to discuss class issues in the United States of America. Or they might feel awkward, or defensive. Those of us from working class families shy from such discussions because we fear rejection, that familiar dismissal of the inferior, people who might not belong in the fabric store. Even more, we fear the accusations of self-pity that come not just from the world at large but from our own inner voices. No matter how much our experience may have belied the myth of equal opportunity, we recognize that unlike race and, usually, gender, social class is something that can change. A woman who has been to college ought to feel comfortable in any restaurant, I had just been scolding myself—as though beneath the soft new shirt of my degrees was not the same skin I had been born with.

Yet I had worked hard as a teacher to break down the barricades of exclusion, not just exclusion by class and race and gender and sexual orientation but by fear, by violence, any limits prescribed by others on the legitimacy of our bodies and our minds and our lives. "Make noise!" I told my students. "Take up space!" Enduring pain in silence was not the template

I wanted them to follow, especially now. When I walked into my first classroom in 1967—eager and scared and having everything to learn about teaching—Martin Luther King Jr. was still alive, and infinite possibilities lay ahead. When I packed the last box of books and papers into my car and drove away from my final classroom in 2002, things looked bleaker. Most of my students were heading to war or to Wal-Mart. The race and gender issues we children of the sixties had thought would surely be resolved within our lifetimes continued to trouble our country, and apparently even I was still not ready to talk openly about class.

Traffic had thinned miles ago; ahead of me now was only open road. I heard the hum of my own tires, then the sudden song of the Western Meadowlark, those bright liquid notes which can easily penetrate glass and metal. "Listen to the quiet!" city dwellers marvel when they vacation in these Oregon mountains and high desert open spaces. But there is much to hear: the river's current, wind in the sage and Ponderosa, the warning call of the quail. The skip of tumble-mustard across hard-packed earth. The sluff of blowing snow, the groan of lake ice. Crows feathering the air. If we would listen this attentively to human silences, could we hear the jostling echoes of each other's lives?

You even became a college teacher. I thought about that circle of desks, students leaning forward to make sure they understood, and then about the people who didn't get to be there. My father, my mother. My grandmother, whose absence had shaped my own life's lessons. So many empty desks. I was one of the lucky ones who had been given this gift, this chance to speak. And stories, I knew, can change us; the storyteller herself might not be quite the same person by the story's end. All I needed was to find the words.

A pair of tumbleweeds bounced across the asphalt and rolled into the sage. I felt my shoulders relaxing, my hands light now on the steering wheel. Even in this desert stillness words were everywhere, familiar as breath: tumbleweed, balancing its name and its life journey, forever looking for a place to belong.

Borders

When Jack Fleming came to Orofino, Idaho, population 1750, in the timber country just south of Idaho's narrow panhandle, I was still in eighth grade. He was here to teach high school, but the principal had assigned him a last-period classroom downstairs in the junior high, so that spring his senior English class shared a wall with the room where we were waiting out the afternoons under the watchful eye of Mrs. Filer. Our own teacher was a strong-armed woman who kept a wooden paddle in her bottom desk drawer, and she could turn around quicker than any hefty person we had ever seen, though we weren't usually up to much when she did. I remember staring past her as if we could see through the blackboard behind her desk. Mr. Fleming was different, people said. There were rumors of big things going on over there. All I knew for sure was that the high school kids on the school bus had the kind of English textbooks I wished we had. They called them "lit" books. Literature. The word was almost too big to hold onto; it pushed against the roof of my mouth like a building thunderhead.

For now, books came from the one-room library across the street from the school. We could check out two at a time, though until we were twelve they had to be books with a "J" on the spine. My sister had taught me to read when I was four, so I had run out of J books long before I was twelve and had to read the best ones over and over, *Caddie Woodlawn* and *Huckleberry Finn*, and *Silver Chief, Dog of the North*. Now Jill and I were both old enough for the adult books, but after I had finished *The Yearling* and *The Red Badge of Courage* I didn't know which ones might turn out to be literature. This one, with the glossy cover? Or the one with the strange title: *Catcher in the Rye*? Whatever I chose, and no matter how disappointing they often turned out to be, by Sunday night I would have read them and Jill's books too, and she would have finished mine as well as hers.

Like starving children, we had always read as if print were edible. One summer when we couldn't get to town we read all the moldy gray and white women's magazines we had found in the tiny board shack beneath the barnyard trees where an aunt had ridden out the Depression, stories about small children racked with sobs because they had to choose whether to live with Mama or Daddy, the sad-looking parents with wide shoulders and lapels and those amazingly thick-heeled shoes. *The Idaho Farmer* and the summer edition of *Weekly Reader* appeared like treasures in the mailbox—sometimes even a check from the *Idaho Farmer's* children's page, where we could earn a dollar for our own stories, mysteries set in old barns or abandoned mine shafts. We trudged up the steep gravel driveway every afternoon to wait for the mail jeep, just in case. Once I opened the box to find a *Junior Natural History Magazine*. The cover showed a boy sitting in an old kitchen chair on a raft, fishing. And it wasn't a mistake; that was my name on the label. Mom smiled as if she were keeping a secret.

If she had her way, I knew, our house would be filled with books. She had wanted to be a nurse, but I always imagined her as a poet-scientist, maybe an astronomer. Dad was smart too, but during the Depression even a high school education was a luxury he couldn't afford. Now the country was in what I would later learn to call post-war recovery, but the economic good times hadn't reached our family. My sister and I hated paydays, and they happened every two weeks: Mom and Dad hunched over the bills at one end of the kitchen table, tense, arguing about the best way to stretch the money. Our family raised a big garden here on Dad's family homestead, eighty acres of steep hillside and a narrow strip of stump-farm benchland, and Mom sewed most of our clothes. But there were bills at the grocery store and the feed store, and three more children in the family now. No matter how hard they worked or how carefully they scrimped, there was never quite enough to pay for our shoes and broken glasses. We heard real anguish in our father's voice when he came home from his job at the lumber mill to learn that Mom had signed a contract committing them to spend $300 on *The Encyclopedia Americana*. "For that kind of money we could have put in a bathroom!" She had bought the children's encyclopedia, too—*The Book of Knowledge*, and a set of science books, and the *Children's Classics: Robinson Crusoe* and *Kidnapped*, *Heidi* and *Robin Hood* and *Black Beauty*. It would take two years to make all the payments. So many mornings when I staggered sleepily past my mother on the way out to do barn chores, she would be propped on a kitchen chair reading the encyclopedia, stealing those moments between seeing our father off to work and getting the my younger brothers up for breakfast in time to catch the bus. She read a chapter from the small shelf of *Children's Classics* out loud every night. Dad's chair faced the other way, but we could tell by the way he held his head that he was listening too.

My classmates and I didn't get to do much reading in eighth grade English; Mrs. Filer's idea of a good English assignment was to have us underline subjects and predicates. Once, though, she let us spend the whole afternoon, our English hour and the last part of science too, writing short stories based on pictures she had cut from magazines and old calendars. When she pulled out that manila folder and started propping up the pictures of ocean beaches and the Grand Canyon on the blackboard sills, a shiver went through the room. Pencils whispered around me as my own words poured into a blue spiral notebook. In my story a boy became an instant hero by stabbing a man-eating octopus in a secret spot—only he knew about it—right behind the eye. Under cover of the ink that shot out, murking the water, he grabbed the other diver and pulled him to the surface, safe as houses. When the bell rang we all jumped. My hand ached from writing so fast. I put my story in the stack of papers on Mrs. Filer's desk as my row filed out the door—folded once, lengthwise, my name in the upper right corner. Had anyone in our class actually seen the ocean? Orofino was part of what the radio announcers called the Inland Empire—not that far from the ocean on the map, but too far to get there and back on your day off. Mrs. Filer would return our papers tomorrow or the next day with a letter grade at the top of the first page, maybe "watch spelling" printed in block letters beside it.

Most days, we were the only story going—we sweaty in-betweens, not grade schoolers and not high schoolers, waiting and waiting for something, whatever was out there though what it might be we didn't know. Runnered rows of ancient wooden desks creaked with our shifting weight and logging trucks roared up Michigan Avenue toward Johnson's Mill. The minute hand on the big white clock above the flag was bent, jerking along far behind each tick.

On the warm April afternoon that Mr. Fleming let the seniors leave a few minutes before the bell rang, every head lifted and all eyes looked toward our own classroom door. Mrs. Filer was already out in the hall. "He turned us loose, lady," we heard somebody say. Then we heard something else, a murmur and the quiet click of a latch. The situation was in hand, she told us when she came back. Yes, Mr. Fleming had dismissed his class, but he wouldn't be doing so again. Just because they're seniors doesn't mean they can get away with that, she said. Other people have work to do even if they don't.

We were only eighth graders so we knew there were days beyond counting until we would have this Mr. Fleming for English, but interest was high. A teacher who thought for himself and taught literature too? Four years was such a long time to wait.

It would have been even harder if we had known what lay ahead. When we were freshmen we would have a math teacher mis-assigned to English because, as everyone knew, women shouldn't try to teach trigonometry. She hated the grammar lessons as much as we did, so I tried to tell her about

15

the old literature books in the storeroom—the ones I had found when I sneaked off with my bathroom hall pass and climbed the stepladder to the top shelf, sitting there above the view of any teacher who happened by. There was one story called "An Occurrence at Owl Creek Bridge," I told her; we could talk about the ending, figure out what it meant. But gerunds and infinitives were already more than she could handle, she said.

Our new sophomore English teacher ate lettuce leaves dipped into a pint jar of milk for lunch. Her thin body was shaped like a question mark: when she walked down the aisle toward the teacher's desk we heard her knees run into it, thunk thunk. "Let's break her in right!" my friend Pam grinned across the back row aisle, but she broke us; we were bark chips on the landing by Christmas break. "Because I Could Not Stop for Death," she wrote in her chalk-wobble writing on the blackboard, and told us to analyze this poem. Were we even close? We would never know; maybe our words had melted into a salad of limp leaves and room-temperature milk. Give a 30-minute report on Edgar Allen Poe; write a summary of 50 Greek myths; read *The Merchant of Venice* from a text with no footnotes. "What does this mean?" we asked our science teacher. "It says here a man is made of metal?" But he just shook his head. "Can you give our papers back sometimes? Can we find out what other people think the stories mean?" I asked her once. "You should be a doctor," she said. No one ever knew why the FBI came looking for her that summer.

Our junior year teacher—well, we knew why the police had wanted him. The only people he fooled, people whispered, were the nine different landlords he had in that school year, the ones who had agreed to accept the rent at the end of 30 days. "Could you criticize my writing sometimes?" I wrote on one of the daily in-class paragraphs. "I'd like to learn to write better." SORRY, he scrawled across the bottom. His black-rimmed glasses reflected the glare of the snow outside the window and I wasn't sure he really had eyes, although of course he must have because he was reading the murder mysteries aloud. Pay attention, he told us. The test would cover the smallest details. We heard he served some time in the Walla Walla State Pen a couple of years after he had been our teacher. Nickel and dime stuff, probably.

So when I was a senior I walked into Jack Fleming's classroom ready. There weren't so many of us now because you didn't have to take senior English unless you wanted to go to college. The principal had moved him upstairs to a corner room where light streamed in from tall northwest windows. "Reading maketh a full man," he said, and sent us home to write our own essays following the sentence patterns in Francis Bacon's "On

Reading." By this time we had heard more stories about Mr. Fleming. He lived in that little one-room cabin above the river, and he walked across the bridge and up the railroad tracks to school. He didn't own a car. No wife, no kids. He wore the same dark sweater every day, and corduroy jeans. All the other men, even the coaches, wore sports jackets and ties. I wondered how they could afford them; they didn't make much more than my dad, who owned only two chambray shirts and two pairs of Wrangler jeans.

"On Religion," I wrote at the top of a blank page. I didn't really mean religion the way other people seemed to mean it—in fact, I had already been told to leave the Wells Bench Community Sunday School and not come back. *To escape God's wrath you must renounce the world!* I had laughed out loud. What I was about to write was risky: I had not forgotten that long walk home, the sound of my shoes in the loose gravel and the smell of dust from the log trucks hanging in the summer air. But I had to find out. Would this quiet, different man who wasn't much for convention read a paper about religion with respect? If teachers can test kids all the time, maybe we could test them back, is what I was thinking.

On Monday he returned our papers, covered with a fine red script—in the margins, between the lines, everywhere. He was talking to us. He was taking us seriously. He thought we were thinkers.

"Interesting topic," he said as he handed me my paper. Just the hint of a smile.

Then Shakespeare's sonnets came alive, line by line, each word holding the world down with its weight. Beowulf. "Christ, that my love were in my arms and I in my bed again!" Look more closely at William Blake, he told us. He drew a circle on the board, wrote INNOCENCE in his square letters above the circle and EXPERIENCE below, and we heard a small boy weeping. "About suffering they were never wrong, the old masters," we read. "When there was peace, he was for peace. When there was war, he went." Mr. Fleming had graduated from the University of Chicago; word was he had grown up in an orphanage back there. That may have been just a story, but he had that kind of toughness, something about his hands, and his eyes. Scanning the perimeter, we would learn to call it all too soon. Sometimes I could tell he still wanted to run from us, his own private congregation of cabbage-heads. Some people dozed. "Onward through the fog," he said, looking down and picking up another piece of broken chalk. "I liked it, but I didn't understand it," I told him when I returned his heavy silver copy of Faulkner's *The Hamlet*. "It's in your mind, though," he said. "It will be there when you need it." Once he caught himself quoting: "The unexamined life is not worth living." Then he looked over at me. "Don't write that down." But I already had.

Two weeks after graduation, he drove up the mountain to bring me more books. "Keep a vocabulary list," he said. "Why are you so set on teaching English? Read this, read Margaret Mead. Look what else there is in the world to do!" Stacks of books. Thomas Haskell. Samuel Johnson. Shaw, and more Shaw. His red Clearwater Timber Protection Association fire-crew pickup churned its way back up our washboard gravel driveway—like all the other teachers, he had to have a summer job—leaving me smiling at his final admonition. "When you get to campus, don't go gawking at the architecture!"

Somehow—it seemed both miraculous and inevitable—I was going to college. According to my entrance exams, I should become an architect. "There are no rules against admitting women to this program," the counselor had told me. "You need to realize, though, that at every level of your career you will be competing with men. It will be an uphill struggle." He wanted me to take another test designed for women. This one said I would find success as a teacher of home economics—the subject I had been dodging all through high school, though it was required for girls. But I already knew that I had no choice. I had to major in English. The University of Idaho didn't have a creative writing program—in fact, I didn't know that such programs existed—but literature was the way into everything I needed to understand before I could begin to write my own stories. On registration day, following Mr. Fleming's advice, I switched from the College of Education to the College of Letters and Science. Standing in line for hours was a cheap price to pay, really. It was literature I wanted to study, not lesson planning.

But I was doing quite a bit of head-tipped-back staring. Gargoyles and buttresses and parapets. The real wonder was my dormitory desk itself, that built-in bookshelf with the first semester's textbooks leaning heavily against one corner. By spring the shelf was almost full. We were reading the *Iliad*, *Madame Bovary*, Lorca's poems. Aeschylus, Sophocles, Euripides. Professor Banks was chuckling when—halfway through our exam—my roommate Eugenie realized that Don Quixote had been badly treated and sputtered, "Damn them! Damn them all!" as she bent over her Blue Book. He was inviting Eugenie and me over for cake and coffee with his wife, who taught literature too; they wanted us to hear their recording of Dylan Thomas reading "Fern Hill." We might miss the sorrow of the poem, he said, unless we could hear Thomas's voice. They took us to see a performance of *Medea*. Were we their god-children, I wondered? They were old, white-haired old, and happy. Their walls were lined with books. Once, when I wrote that I thought I could never catch up with everything I needed to know, he scribbled a note to me in the margin, "Plan to live a few more years." That spring he read my first story to the class while we sat outside on the grass. I lay back and stared at the sky, hardly able to breathe. But they liked it. On the final exam he left me another note in his shaky, back-slanted handwriting: *It is a pleasure to travel along beside you and shout like an excited guide into the depths of your awareness.*

The College of Letters and Science would be giving me a Bachelor of Arts degree in English, but I would have to take enough education courses to qualify for a teaching certificate. Eugenie and I made a game of it, counting the times the professor started a sentence with the words "Now I'd like to go ahead and say..." Once he read aloud my parody of his lecture on Horace Mann; I had written a perfect midterm exam, he said, an example for others to follow. Eugenie tried not to look at me; we had to pass the class if we were going to be able to support ourselves after graduation.

"What will you do if you don't make it as a teacher?" another friend had asked me the summer before my senior year. We were driving her father's truck up to Mill Creek, carrying salt blocks for the cattle on their summer range. She was studying medical technology though she had really wanted to be a vet. Not many women would be admitted to the College of Veterinary Medicine.

"I don't know." I didn't want to say it out loud, but I was scared. What else could you do with an English major? I still wanted to be a writer, but I hadn't even read all of Faulkner yet, much less Joyce. "You'll do okay," she said. When I finally got to my student teaching assignment, though, only the students in the front desks could hear my voice. "Project," frowned my supervisor from the back row. And after the first full day of teaching at White Swan High School—I lived in the back of Harold's General Merchandise and Post Office that year, on the Yakama Indian Reservation—I kicked off my shoes and let my skirt fall in a heap around my feet. The waistband was damp with sweat. Nine months, counting weekends. One hundred and seventy-nine more days: I had signed a contract.

But the kids were far better teachers than the education professors. Or the principal, whose advice had been to seat students alphabetically and make sure they put their papers on top of the stack as they passed their work up the row. "Miss Lynch, you'll have more luck if you let people write during class," a boy told me one morning before anyone else had arrived. "Most of us have to work after school." When the hop harvest was over and they could start fall term, the four Gonzales girls invited me to their home for a feast that lasted until almost midnight. At eight the next morning we were in class with our writing journals, listening to music on the portable record player Mom had given Jill and me for Christmas when we were in high school. "Don't it always seem to go, that you don't know what you've got 'til it's gone?" Penny Lane, Eleanor Rigby, Mr. Tambourine Man. A boy came up to whisper please don't play that song, the one that says I am a rock, I am an island, because his brother died, his brother had killed himself . . . . Another day someone brought a brand new album called *Alice's Restaurant*, and I watched as pens stopped moving and heads came up to listen. "It's the Alice's Restaurant anti-massacree movement, and all you've got to do to join is sing it the next time it comes around on the guitar!" During the break between classes they spread the word; Arlo Guthrie was the poet we would hear all day. "Kid, we don't like your kind..." We listened to each other's voices, *The Diary of Anne Frank, Twelve Angry Men*. I had only one copy of *All Quiet on the Western Front*, so I read it aloud to the sophomores. How many of them would live through Viet Nam? I didn't know if it would help or not. A shadow-eyed boy who lived out in Medicine Valley rarely came to school but every time he did I gave him another book, *One Flew Over the Cuckoo's Nest* or *To Kill a Mockingbird* or *All the King's Men*, and he disappeared for three more days. One morning I played a chorus by the Clancy Brothers:

> *When we were savage, fierce and wild*
> *(Whack fol the diddle fol the di do day)*
> *She came as a mother to her child,*
> *(Whack fol the diddle fol the di do day)*
> *Gently raised us from the slime*
> *And kept our hands from hellish crime—*
> *And sent us to heaven in her own good time!*
> *(Whack fol the diddle fol the di do day)*

Bill, a slender Yakama boy whose wrist bent so gracefully when he arced a shot toward the basket but who was always so quiet in class, tipped his head back and laughed out loud.

Maybe this was why Mr. Fleming had warned me about becoming a teacher. Once you started, it was hard to stop.

Twenty-five years after high school graduation I was back in my hometown, broke and without a classroom after budget cuts in the school district where I had been teaching, and Jack Fleming was managing the Sunset Mart gas station. He had lost that sweater but otherwise he looked exactly the same. He still moved on his feet like a boxer. Once I had seen him jackknife off the board at Bruce's Eddy and breaststroke across the North Fork of the Clearwater. "Didn't you know he was a championship diver in college?" somebody had said. But that white sand beach was washing under 400 feet of dammed water now.

Some major concrete had been poured across my channel, too. The battered old GMC that I had driven into the station said LAST CHANCE GARAGE on the door and someone had smeared a mock racing stripe down its side with a yellow paintbrush. Yes, I told him, I was writing, though I hadn't had any poems accepted by the major journals. *"Try Ploughshares,"* he said. "They took one of mine last winter." He's still a teacher, I thought.

But the present seemed less open to possibility. I counted out the money for the gas, and he picked up a white bucket of frozen fries and carried them around the corner. What was he doing here? Making ends meet on his retirement income, I supposed—but what had he ever been doing in our little raw pine town in the shadows of this Idaho canyon?

The next time my truck needed gas he reached under the counter and brought up a brown grocery bag filled with *American Poetry Review* magazines. "Read these," he said. "These are very helpful."

I left town again in the middle of a January blizzard to start my next teaching job, part time at Blue Mountain Community College in Pendleton. Five thousand dollars a year. I had those poems packed in the back seat and just enough in the tank to get me across the border to Oregon. Two years later, when I went back to Idaho to visit my family, Jack Fleming was gone. He had eventually married the landlady who owned that cabin and now the marriage had broken up, and whatever mystery had held him in our little logging town upriver from everywhere had dissolved. I heard one more story about him, though. He had sent a poem to the university's literary journal and the editor had sent it back with a critique written beside each line. "So I found one of his poems and did the same for him," he told someone.

On my way back to Oregon I thought, yes, there is more to do in the world than teach. When Martin Luther King stood on those famous steps the summer that our class graduated from high school and sent shimmers of possibility out over a crowd cheering so loudly we could hear them in Idaho—*I have been to the mountaintop*—I knew things were changing, big things. Teaching was one of the three fields already open, within limits, to women; even then I had understood why Mr. Fleming had higher hopes for me. Yet here I was, with the rolling Palouse wheat fields leaning from green to gold all around me, on my way back to yet another classroom. I had a full-time job again, but how long it would last was anybody's guess, and I had lost my home and my savings. Not to mention all those other possible versions of my life. I didn't envy Margaret Mead, but what about Jane Goodall, or those wind-burned young naturalists who study orcas and terns? What about Annie Dillard?

Once a small red car had pulled up beside me at a traffic light. It was a bit battered-looking, daisies and hand-lettered slogans painted on the doors and fenders. "Have you shared a book today?" "Reading is a piece of cake!" As the driver moved ahead in the other lane, her primary message spread in huge letters across the back bumper: READING SAVES LIVES. Another teacher, Title I probably, on her way to work.

That week my American Literature class had been listening to a taped interview with Maxine Hong Kingston. "Are you the Woman Warrior?" the interviewer wanted to know. No, Kingston had answered. *The Woman Warrior* had been an unfortunate title, really, for her first book. The warrior/storyteller's words—carved in blood on the narrator's back, the words this woman warrior bears as scars—are small, really, compared to one bomb. One grenade. "Writers maybe conquer a reader at a time," Kingston said in her soft voice. "We change the atmosphere of the world—we change moods here and there—whereas the people who have the guns and the bombs...if only the word had as much power..."

Yet the metaphor she wanted us to remember was storytelling, not war.

"How important are stories?" I had asked my students when we turned off the tape player. "Compared to, say, the stock market? Or stealth bombers?" They already knew that I considered *The Woman Warrior*—all the American Literature readings, for that matter—sacred texts. *Tell Me a Riddle. After Sand Creek.* "Sonny's Blues." Even I might not call Cabeza de Vaca's journals sacred, they could probably have guessed—or Bradford's Puritan history, even if it was intended to be a revered cornerstone of the City on the Hill for God's chosen people—but what all these texts do, they had heard me argue, is at least as important as the Psalms. They make us question our assumptions. They put us in the center of our lives. They make us lost, and completely human.

To many people, though, a literature class was simply one way to fulfill the humanities credit requirement. Maybe the ones who answer, I had cautioned myself, will simply be trying to please me.

"This class saved my life," one woman said. She didn't seem to know what to say next, but a man nodded, and then I heard another quiet murmur somewhere to my right. Something they had read or something they had heard in a class discussion had pulled them out of a hole I could only imagine, lifting them over the barricades of their current lives, maybe over the gates of some limitation they had been trapped in since childhood. But other students were looking at their watches: it was already time for them to go—to their next class, to their jobs at the Wal-Mart Distribution Center, to pick up their children.

"I need to talk to you—I know my paper's late. This book really got to me," John told me as the others left the room. His hand trembled when he handed me his paper on Leslie Silko's *Ceremony*. "I'm sorry I missed class last week," he said. "I was—I couldn't come." He waited, glancing over at the last group of students going out the door. "I was physically detained," he whispered. When he smiled he looked even younger than his nineteen years. In our class discussions he was the one who had noticed that when Silko's main character tries to escape into alcohol, the forces of destruction exert their power.

I would not see him again. "I know John didn't finish your class," his sister told me later. "He barely started it. But I think it helped him. He's been working some things out." She wanted to become an English teacher too—high school, or maybe college. Should I warn her: Don't do it, don't let yourself hope for a miracle this personal, this specific? We can give our students only what our own teachers have given us. Will it be enough? Will it change anything?

The highway dipped now into the gully where that broken-shingled barn had slumped to its knees under last winter's snow. A great blue heron rose up from Pataha Creek, flying alongside my car, her long neck reaching for something. Herons can be guides, I knew. I leaned forward, arcing my arms over the steering wheel to stretch my back as the heron lifted above the windshield, beyond the scope of my vision. "See how the sudden / gray-blue sheets of her wings / strive toward the wind; see how the clasp of nothing / takes her in," the poet Mary Oliver had described such a moment.

> It isn't a miracle
> but the common thing,
> this decision,

this trailing of the long legs in the water,
this opening up of the heavy body...

Most of the books from my first year of college were still in my mother's bookcase—I took them home to her that summer. She had finally let go of that old encyclopedia set, but even so it had become hard to find space for all the books we were sharing now, books by Barry Lopez and Edward Hoagland and John McPhee, Grace Paley, Lucille Clifton. And Annie Dillard, who like me was born on the last day of April in 1945, the day that the man who had led the world into the crystalline madness of walled ghettoes and barbed wire prisons and killing chambers with no exits retreated to an underground bunker, put a pistol to his temple, and pulled the trigger. Annie Dillard and I were eight days old on the May morning when the Allied troops arrived at Bergen-Belsen. People of our generation will always measure the truth of any assertion about human behavior against those photographs. And the babies born on the day Hitler died were three months old when "Big Boy" and "Little Boy" were dropped on the children of Japan. *I have become death, the destroyer of worlds.* An instructor at the Air Force Academy, according to Kingston's *Fifth Book of Peace*, now assigns *The Woman Warrior* to inspire female cadets to military prowess. Kingston has asked him not to interpret the book that way, explaining that she meant the story to have the opposite meaning, but he is adamant. He finds the book useful. "I have to live with that," she writes.

My hands were gripping the steering wheel so hard that my wrists ached. I wanted to see Jack Fleming again. Had he tried to talk me out of becoming a teacher because he already knew that it might not be possible, his vision that now I, too, had spent so many years pursuing in my own classrooms? "Remember that word you suggested for my graduation speech?" I wanted to ask him. What possibilities, in these times of pre-emptive war, for 'interdependence'? What possibilities, with this widening gap between the rich and poor, for closing the old wounds of race, gender, social class? Can we keep from trapping ourselves inside these wounds? What is wealth, what does it mean? Who gets to hear which stories?"

Soon I would be opening the door of a warm September classroom to a new group of students. Now, I would tell them—keeping my fingers crossed inside the pocket of my khakis, a plea as well as a blessing—

I will you to be a bold swimmer

To jump off in the midst of the sea, and rise again and nod to me and shout, and laughingly dash with your hair...

I wanted a miracle for each of them, that boy in the baseball cap, the woman whose hands would be trembling in her lap. To discover what is possible. To be more fully themselves, more fully human. But how far out from the shores of my childhood had I managed to swim myself? While a young Annie Dillard was writing *Pilgrim at Tinker Creek* I had been learning to use the movie projector at White Swan High School and checking books out of another one-room library, this one open only on Tuesday and Thursday nights.

I had saved almost half of the money I earned at that first teaching job to go on to graduate school. And I got a fellowship through the National Defense Education Act. Two hundred dollars a month! After I had received my master's degree in English I stayed in school, taking courses in Seventeenth Century Poetry, Comparative Literature. William Carlos Williams, Walt Whitman, Emily Dickinson. Courses I had not been able to take because of that missing semester when I had to leave campus to do my practice teaching. But I did not finish the Ph.D. "It's a shame that a woman of your abilities won't be able to find a university position," one of my professors at the University of Colorado told me after he'd had a few drinks. Yes, that was part of it, no question. But the director of the graduate English program had already asked each of us to state our academic goals, and by the time the circle had come around to my end of the seminar table my voice had been shaking. "I might return to high school teaching." The director had looked away.

I was as smart as the others, whether he thought so or not: I had earned my Bachelor's degree with a perfect 4.0 grade average, only the twelfth student in the history of my university to do that—the second woman— and I was doing well in grad school. But something was missing, the social syntax, what I would later learn to call the arc of the story. Could intelligence alone lift me to the two-story house on a hill above some university campus, my own walls lined with books? I didn't know how far I could ride this wave. I might float into that liminal space between worlds and lose my place at the table of the working class. Where would I belong?

I reached down to turn on the radio. For a few miles I let violins struggle through patches of static. Finally I pushed the button for silence. You were young, I told myself. You'd make different choices now. Light was fading from the eastern rim of the Blue Mountains, the sky just above the distant Lodgepoles a pale lavender. "Coming to college isn't just about getting a better job," I often told my students. "That's good, that's wonderful, maybe it's what got you in the door. And it will probably happen. But the real reason you are here, no matter what they tell you at the Admissions Office, is to change your lives. To learn. To discover ideas that will—"

Teaching is a passion, like writing itself. And it takes much of the same energy, all that focus on other people's words. But for a long time now I had been getting up every morning at four, and by the time I got to class I was dazed, lost in that place where writers go. Students looked at me, wondering what it was all about. Some of them already knew. "Even race and gender issues seem easier to approach than the issues of class we are all struggling with on a daily basis, don't they?" I said. "But you can't really talk about one without including the others, the strands are braided so closely that the dyes bleed into each other..."

I wondered if I would ever see Jack Fleming again. Maybe my words will find him, I thought. I could almost imagine him holding my stories, his eyes scanning the page. When the highway dipped down to the Umatilla another heron startled into flight, leading me across the river into Pendleton, the place where—hungry and desperate—I had at last become a college teacher.

Eating

I have returned to the Blue Sky Restaurant several times since the hot pepper incident. Once I shared a casual fish taco dinner with another group of friends—the restaurant, to my happy surprise, had redefined itself under new management. But the next time those white tablecloths were back, and the new chef, a young man with a wild mop of hair, was so pleased by praise from someone at our table that he kept sending us sample plates of his best work, sprays and twists of foods I couldn't recognize. When I tried to pay for our meals—the management did not accept credit cards and I was the only one who carried cash—I didn't have enough money. Prices had quadrupled since the fish taco supper.

Now the space that was once the Blue Sky has become a bakery. Townspeople line up at 8 a.m. for warm loaves of amazing, wholesome breads. When we make our yearly pilgrimage to the ocean, Dean and I get there early, too; we like to take our prize down to the beach and tear it apart with our hands. Brown grains, just-sweet with honey and salt air. I'm a long way from Forney Hall, I think on those mornings.

➤·❧·⦿·❧·❧

Get your elbows off the table, Bette Lynch
Get your elbows off the table, Bette Lynch
Get your elbows off the table
Just as soon as you are able
Get your elbows off the table, Bette Lynch!

Of course I had jerked them hard into my lap at the first line of the song, my face burning through the "Round the table you must go!" chorus. It was a joke, I knew—even a compliment of sorts, kidding a senior like this. Still, in four years I had never heard them do it to anyone else. Relaxed at last in my college dormitory dining hall, I'd had no idea my habits were this notorious—or even that I had such habits. They had to catch me at lunch because I ate dinner in the kitchen, jammed elbow to elbow with the sweaty young men who washed dishes and carried trays and scoured the grill. We climbed over the metal seat to claim any available spot at the bench table; usually, though, if I were wearing a slim skirt the others would slide down to give me a place on the end. Our food was bathed in steam and the odors of grease and ammonia—the workers' table stretched between the coffee machines and the stainless steam tables, dishwashing machines churning just behind us. We had already started our shifts, but we had to clock out for this meal. Sometimes people pushed someone else's time card into the machine as well as their own when they returned to work, but if the dietician noticed it would cost both people their jobs. Most of us just ate quickly. Then, for me, it was back to setting up dessert trays. On easy nights, dessert was something like cake or pudding or the much-despised Plum Torte. More often my job was dipping into vats of strawberry or vanilla ice cream hard enough for the first servings to stay frozen as I filled all 180 bowls and slid them into clockwise circles on the trays.

Beyond the swinging double doors just past the time clock, dining was more formal. Hostesses and sub-hostesses at every table, with special rules for passing rolls or salt and pepper shakers (take them in your right hand, index finger between them; transfer them to the palm of your left hand, and holding them close to your body, offer them to the girl on your right; the basket of rolls followed the same procedure but you had to remember which hand uncovered the rolls for your neighbor, which hand re-covered them before passing, and which hand actually passed the basket). In fact, there were special rules for each food, it had seemed to me as a freshman. There wasn't quite enough room for three chairs along the sides of the tables so one person's chair was a bit too far from her plate, with canyons of space for cubes of lime Jell-o to splat into if her fork trembled. Was a fork right for Jell-o cubes? I watched the others to be sure. Dress dinner every Wednesday night, hose and heels, and of course on Sunday afternoons when we sang the Doxology and then sat down—racing to pull in our chairs now—to small ginger ale and sherbet cocktails placed on paper doilies. "Stir three times only, and stir to the right," the Etiquette Chair had scolded us during the weekly meetings she required of all freshmen.

"You'll get used to it," a girl I had known in high school said one night, her voice too low for the others to hear. Was my discomfort this visible? Like every child I knew, I'd grown up with what our mothers called good table manners; I loved holiday meals when Mom let me polish her wedding-present silverware, the special knife just for butter. We had practiced formal table settings in 4-H. But this was a different world altogether—not just something more to learn, but disturbing in a way I didn't understand. "Don't throw y'r bones under the table," Dad wrote after I had fired home my first astonished letter. "They may not have a dog."

And maybe he was right: it was better to laugh about it. After all, eating hadn't always been a problem. I thought about the shelves in my family's cellar, that rainbow of colors they would be carrying up out of that darkness: beets and green beans in pint-sized Mason jars, peaches and apricots in quarts; and red-flecked and purple cherries, too. Plums. Corn, and more corn. Hubbard squashes heaped against the burlap bags of potatoes, Reds and Russets. Onions. Carrots, still nearly crisp. Blackberry jam, strawberry, raspberry. Pints of apple butter. Quart after quart of applesauce. Pears. Dill pickles, bread-and-butter pickles. Cabbages and kings.

"Are we poor?" my sister and I had once asked our mother. We were in grade school then, trying to sort out a confusing world. "No," she said. "Poor families don't have warm coats in the winter time, or good food to give their children." Her voice sounded strange, almost as if she were about to cry.

In the refrigerator thick cream rose to the top of the milk jars. Brown and white eggs, mounds of butter. Mom made bread twice a week, five loaves at a time, with a pan of rolls for supper. There was always a hot crust if you were drawn by the smell; sometimes she'd divide a whole loaf into crusts, laughing as both top and bottom and then the side crusts became heels too, and all that remained was a steaming white chunk of soft bread shaped like a Velveeta cheese box. Some things came from the Corner Store, of course: navy beans and pectin and celery, flour in 50 pound cloth sacks, sugar in 25 pound paper ones. Corn flakes and Shredded Wheat, with Straight Arrow's directions for fire-making printed on the cardboard dividers; eating three of what looked like bowl-sized bales of hay, Mom promised, could earn me access to all this wisdom. We had to buy nutmeg, and brown sugar, vanilla, ginger, molasses and cinnamon. Sometimes even bananas—purchased two at a time and divided for several of us to share; or maybe you were the lucky one who got the end pieces when a whole banana fell, slice after slice, into the cream pie filling. But the meat—venison, chicken, bacon and pork chops and this fall's beef unless the milk cow had produced a heifer and not a steer last year—came from home. Visiting uncles loosened their belts and asked for a third helping of those homemade noodles. Then cinnamon rolls, or huckleberry pie, or white cake made with six egg whites. For how many winter lunches—it's such a common memory—had we skipped the soup or sandwiches and just eaten oatmeal cookies with our bowls of apricots or Royal Anne cherries swimming in their juice?

There had been hints, though. At Thanksgiving and Christmas we had the ham Dad brought home from the mill, tucked under the arm of his work jacket. "My Christmas bonus," he called it; a bitter joke I hadn't completely understood. It had something to do with the fact that we were supposed to be eating turkey like the family in the Norman Rockwell painting. But one day the mail-lady had driven her jeep right down the driveway and stayed to watch while Mom opened the package from Montgomery Ward. Dark blue/green plates, a dusty pink rose in each center. Cups and saucers too. And gold rims. I knew it wasn't real gold but it couldn't have been prettier if it were. For a while, at least, we had all had the same plates, just like the families in the pictures.

"I came to the university to study English Literature," Eugenie announced after a few weeks of etiquette lessons. "Not this Emily Post crap." Hadn't our mothers been right? Good manners, they had taught us, simply meant behaving with courtesy, making other people feel comfortable. When the Etiquette Chair—"Mary Manners," we called her—complained that excessive stirring of the Sunday cocktails was creating a noise she would not tolerate, we laughed, and we couldn't stop laughing. Was it our fault, as the upper-class women implied, that Mary went home before the semester ended? A nervous breakdown, they called it. It was a serious question, enough to give us pause.

But our studies were serious too. Both of us were elated to be, finally, at the university, trying to make sense of James Joyce and Wallace Stevens, shaking each other awake, "Listen to this! *washed by time's waters as they rose and fell / about the stars and broke in days and years...* It's Yeats, isn't he amazing?" We wanted to cheer when Dr. Seaman streamed into our philosophy class in his scarlet-lined black cape. Cambium cells that seemed identical but magically could become either xylem or phloem, either bark or wood, appeared under botany class microscopes; turquoise tarn lakes lit the huge screen in the geology lecture hall. Zoroastrians split the world with their mental razors, British kings stood in a wobbly row like faded dominoes. There was so much to learn, and never quite enough time. Yet we had to spend precious hours every day perfecting rituals designed to impress our future husband's business associates—in the home we would be sharing with whatever boy might "pin" us—though who could imagine tapping a water glass to summon one's own white-jacketed waiter for another slice of Wonder Bread?

In the world beyond our own, people our age were dying in Viet Nam and already beginning to spread Flower Power in San Francisco. But the University of Idaho still claimed an obligation—*in loco parentis*, the Forney Hall handbook described it—to women students, so we were locked inside our dorms at night and subjected to bed checks, Saturday morning room inspections complete with demerits, and the threat of "campusing"—being grounded to our desks for the weekend. Why should the dining room regulations bother us even more than these other insults? It would be years before Eugenie and I would be able to articulate the answer. We weren't sure what meals were like in the sorority houses where the more affluent girls lived, but our dining room's practices were daily reminders of what felt to us like an official state belief in our inferior status. Dormitory girls, the daughters of mill workers and house painters, were apparently the metaphorical equivalent of rough-out leather: with enough polish we might be able to pass as smooth.

It was this smoldering but unspoken resentment that got me into trouble over something that I didn't think would have anything to do with eating. In the spring of my freshman year, I was tapped for Spurs. I had seen them, sophomores visible as angels every Thursday as they walked across the Administration Building lawn toward their classes dressed in white, pleated woolen skirts and V-necked sweaters with a golden spur emblem stitched across the front. All I knew about them, though, was that they handed out programs at the football games (our attendance was required, Mary Manners had insisted). "It's a service organization," someone explained after I was pulled out of bed to join an excited early morning parade of pajama-clad freshmen. "The Spur keeps her residence connected to what's happening on campus." I must have looked less than enthused. "It would let down everyone in Forney Hall if you didn't join," this girl insisted. "It's a terrific honor; everyone wants to be a Spur."

All though initiation week I scraped a silver cowboy spur along the sidewalk, determined to get into the spirit of the thing. I was already president of our dorm's Freshman Honorary, which had turned out to mean only that it was my job to refill the basement pop machine on Saturday mornings; if more of my services had been requested, of course I would comply. On Thursday afternoon we initiates met in a sorority living room to hold delicate teacups and learn the secret Spurs handshake and motto—*Noblesse oblige.* Noblesse oblige? My hometown friend Linda assured me that though the motto was a bit much, the organization was a good thing; she had been a Spur for Alpha Chi. At the group's second meeting, wearing the sweater that had once belonged to Linda, I heard the girl who represented the Tri-Delts propose that we eat dinner at each other's residences after our meetings. "It would be fun," she smiled, "and a good way to get to know each other. Become a real sisterhood! We might even try eating at some of the dorms."

I was close to the door, so I don't think anyone actually noticed when I left. Back in my room, still feeling as if I had swallowed a chunk of basalt, I cut the spur emblem from the sweater and stuffed it into an envelope with my resignation letter. I had made a mistake, that's all. I didn't belong, didn't even want to belong. But of course it was far from over. One of my childhood friends, a girl who had been assigned to the new high-rise dorm where men and women ate together cafeteria-style, turned and walked away when she saw me on campus. "You've disgraced our whole town," she said over her shoulder.

⋗┄◆┄●┄◆┄⋖

Years later, when the community college where I taught plunged into the education-as-a-product business model, a woman was so frustrated by my opposition that she demanded, "Bette, couldn't you just pretend to believe?" Her question took me back to our Forney Hall days, when pretending to believe was the norm, the way into accepting our status. Eugenie and I kept our sanity by making a pretense of pretense. Every dress-dinner Wednesday I wore the same Navy check seersucker suit—four dollars on a sale table at Penney's—with my high school 4-H Beef Production Award pinned to the lapel. Eugenie had made a plan to avoid the dreaded assigned seating at the housemother's table, a scheme as simple as Br'er Rabbit's. Volunteer. For three weeks in a row we gathered with our cohorts around Mrs. Cummerford instead of dodging the Dining Room Girl who waited nightly to snag anyone who met her eye and steer them toward the housemother's head table. "What a beautiful suit," Mrs. Cummerford had said for three consecutive Wednesdays. "Is it new?"

"Yes, thank you," I always answered, looking directly at her.

"And that lovely pin—what does it stand for?"

"Beef. Beef production."

"My. So impressive. I don't begin to understand these things." Mrs. C shared her smile around the table.

There were, we were discovering, rituals within rituals.

Our secret weapon was Joanna Bishop. A tiny thing—"a slip of a girl," Dad would have called her—she looked like a child sitting there beside Mrs. Cummerford. Joanna had recently transferred from the junior college, and it had not taken us long to notice that despite her size, she ate more than any three of us combined, and she ate more slowly than anyone we had ever known. Our plan was simple: at lunchtime, people could leave the dining room as soon as everyone at their table had finished—the only acknowledgment Forney Hall made to a university class schedule—but the rules of dinner etiquette demanded that the housemother's table leave first. No one in the dining room could leave until Joanna had finished eating.

It took three weeks, but Mrs. Cummerford finally surrendered. We got the message through the Dining Room Girl, who didn't even bother with pretense. "You're off the hook," she said. "For good. She says don't ever sit at her table again."

Years later, when I was teaching mythology classes, I read about the Wise Fool: the trickster who emerges from inside the too-tight restrictions of an established society, breaking open the culture so it can grow again. Is that what Eugenie and I had been doing? Or had we just been prolonging our childhoods, playing at satire as the safest way to reclaim our self-worth? If we went too far, we knew, we'd lose the privilege of living in the dorm. Unmarried women had to live on campus, so that would mean expulsion from the university itself.

After graduation, when I could no longer rely on the camaraderie of youthful rebellion, laughter no longer came easily. American culture celebrates ethnic and regional differences in food habits, from Creole gumbo and Maine lobster to "gooey-ducks," those delicious goeduck clams of the Pacific Northwest—but we judge each other by what we eat and how we eat it, too. Of all the areas where I still feel class sensitivities tracking across my life like muddy shoes, eating is the most obvious. Small black checkmarks mar the index in my copy of *The Joy of Cooking*: these, my boyfriend in graduate school said, were the right recipes, the ones with taste. He did not mean the way the food tasted, although, if my stomach was not clenching, it was usually quite good. This kind of marmalade was right, not that kind. Spread on Pepperidge Farm white bread, toasted. Not homemade. When he bought a Thanksgiving turkey large enough to share with other grad students—his family traditionally ate this meal from the Yale plates, he said—I turned for guidance to Rimbauer and Becker. "Make a roux," those wise women advised me.

I closed the book. I do not belong in this apartment, I thought.

That spring an April snowstorm would blow in another man, one who loved baking powder biscuits. We loaded up my blue Falcon and headed off into our lives. For several months while we looked for jobs Dean and I lived on popcorn and pinto beans, both prepared in the cast iron fry pan on a stove someone had abandoned because the only part that worked was one back burner.

"You and Dean are the only people I know who still cook," a friend told me not long ago. I was quartering potatoes for supper. "And you sit down at a table. Amazing."

"How do other people do it?" I asked her. Everyone has to eat...? Somehow I was wrong again, but as usual I had no idea why. "Most people buy prepared food," she explained.

"Left to your own devices," Dean grins at me, "you'd eat nothing but yogurt and berries and Grape Nuts."

"And chocolate," I tell him.

"And that sticks-and-rocks bread," he concedes. "And bananas."

In truth, one of us cooks a meal every night, but what we both seem to want are simple foods. Soups and stews, chicken browned over the electric grill. Beans. Fish. Potatoes and brown rice, steamed vegetables, or even easier, raw ones. I must have cooked more elaborately when our son was growing up; I still have a drawer full of recipes. People marveled at my skills with pie crusts and breads—baking was the only kind of cooking I had learned to do at home, since I was busy at mealtimes with morning and evening barn chores—so it seemed natural to try pita breads and bagels, homemade pretzels and doughnuts. But now crock-pot split pea soup beckons me. Biscuits or corn bread? I ask Dean, knowing the answer. Lemon meringue pie on his birthday. Chocolate cake when I get hungry for it, or Mom's chocolate chip cookies. They were her mother's favorites, too. Three fourths cup brown sugar, three-fourths cup white sugar, two eggs... I will remember these ingredients long after I have forgotten my social security number.

Simplicity, simplicity, simplicity. Keep your recipes on your thumbnail. It's not so much a matter of philosophy, though, as taste. What could be better than a slice of sweet pink grapefruit in December? Or a Braeburn apple? Or a beet, fresh from someone's garden and eaten, still dripping with steam, over the sink? There's a set of plates and bowls in the cupboard, but we don't own china or silver. What are we waiting for? we sometimes ask ourselves. Our fiftieth anniversary? We bought another set of flatware last year but somehow we have ended up with just six teaspoons, no two alike. Good kitchen knives would make all the difference, we agree. Still, they never quite rise to the top of our list.

Sherman Alexie, the Spokane / Coeur d'Alene writer and filmmaker, showed up at our house just weeks before his first book was featured on the front page of the *New York Times Book Review* and he suddenly became famous. He was only 25 that spring, and he had driven down from Spokane to read at the community college in the battered '65 Malibu he would later feature in his first film. ("It made it!" he told someone on the other end of the line when he called home.) When we offered a plate at our table, leftovers stretched with mushroom soup and poured over noodles—it was the day before payday—he was pleased. "Just like an Indian family—You hungry? Sit down, have some of what we're eating!"

It's another kind of belonging, this fellowship of the empty pocket. The cousins recognize each other at first glance. I was still new enough at the college that I had not learned to fight for housing and a department dinner with visiting writers, as well as a much larger honorarium. Maybe it was just as well. Alexie carried his clean jeans and T-shirt in an Albertsons shopping bag. He wouldn't mind that our spare bed was in the converted garage, our son's old sled leaning against the stacks of cardboard boxes. Once, he told me on our way to the reading, his family had lived on a sack of potatoes they found on the roadside.

My students loved Alexie's stories. Most non-Natives in my classes didn't seem to find his world all that different from their own. If I wanted my students to understand Virginia Woolf, though—by now we were discussing her protest against the lack of equal education for women—I would have to begin, again, with food. Even the boiled beef dish she encounters in the women's dining hall and describes with gentle force as "Not Good"—though the water pitcher was passed liberally around the table to accompany it— doesn't sound so bad to my students, who are living on Ramen noodles and the 99 cent fast food specials. They show up for student government barbeques even if they do begin at three in the afternoon, and the baked potato night (signs plastered all over campus: FREE FOOD!) attracted a crowd that ate heartily and left before the Family Night Games for All Ages could get underway.

I have launched into a description of a typical male student's room at Cambridge or Oxford—this is in contrast with the women's fare, I keep telling my students—wine and pheasant under glass; eaten, of course, in front of one's own fireplace, they are all laughing and nodding, yes, now they see what she's saying, when it occurs to me that I don't really have any idea what I'm talking about. Where did I get all this stuff? The movies?

Like most people, I suppose, I learned most of what I really know about food from my mother. The summer that she worked in the hospital as Tray Girl—the summer of 1933—she gained fifteen pounds. Exhausting work and sixteen hour days, but there was cream and butter, milk-rich puddings. She earned fifty cents a day: she could buy her school books and shoes and a coat and two dresses, and get her teeth fixed too. "I put a beautiful beige-flowered dress on lay-away at the Mercantile," she told me, "but by the time I got it paid for it was too small. I loaned it to my sister, but for some reason she gave it to a friend so by Christmas time when I was thin again, it was gone. I never even got to wear it."

"You had lost fifteen pounds by Christmas?" I asked. "Did you diet?"

"Oh no—it didn't take long once I was eating at home. All Mama could make for dinner that winter was potatoes or boiled beans. It was a hungry time."

The Depression's hungry times stretched into years. Mom's brothers found jobs delivering papers, setting pins in the bowling alley, anything they could do. When he was sixteen Fred moved in with a friend across the street to pay his own way, and every morning he stopped by the house with a pint bottle of milk for his youngest sister. "It sounds like a little thing," my Aunt Carolyn remembered once, her voice breaking. "But it wasn't. It wasn't."

Enough to eat. In my own childhood, I could take that for granted. Still, there were times. Like the kerosene beef—that summer the steer had bloated so badly Dad's home remedies couldn't save him, even the desperate last resort of kerosene poured down the animal's throat to induce a belch—and because his children needed this meat he pretended he couldn't taste anything out of the ordinary, or smell the heavy air hanging over the kitchen table. We'd had a meatless winter the year I was in sixth grade, when all the stock had to be sold to pay medical bills and most of the deer had winterkilled the year before, and I was old enough to understand what my father was trying to do. But I couldn't do it, not even for him. Finally it was fall and he was able to shoot a deer, and Mom cleaned the kerosene smell out of the freezer. No one mentioned the beef again.

"I just can't bring myself to sell food," my mother told me one afternoon. The late November light was already fading as she turned back from the window and sat back down beside me at the kitchen table, her face anguished.

Why had I even suggested such a thing? I knew better. The eggs from my chickens could be sold, of course; I cleaned their pen every Saturday and took the cartons of extra eggs to the Corner Store, saving the quarters and dollar bills in a Band-Aid box to pay for my 4-H steer feed. After the county fair when the animals had been purchased by local businessmen (my friend Pam's father bought mine, and when I stayed overnight her mom tried to pretend the meat on my plate had come from deeper in the freezer but I couldn't swallow it, it was Tex and we all knew it), I used the money to buy a cow. All of this was a way of paying for college, the only way I could think of since I couldn't get to town. But it wasn't going to be enough—I'd have two cows and four calves by the time I graduated from high school if I didn't lose a calf to illness or a cow to calving difficulties, not quite enough to pay for my freshman year at the university.

Maybe, I had thought, we could plant another acre of garden. "But fruits and vegetables are different, Bette," Mom was explaining. True enough—I had seen it all my life. People saved extra cream in a tall metal can and turned it into a few precious coins at the Creamery; you could haul any animal in the back of a pickup down to the sales yard, but if you had more apples than you could keep up with you called your neighbor, someone who otherwise wouldn't have applesauce that winter.

By the time spring arrived, though, Mom said she had thought it over and maybe my idea had been a good one after all. It wasn't fair, she said, for us kids not to have any way of earning money. The extra corn rows stretched out into the pasture. It was like a truck garden, wasn't it? I hoed and hoped, and by August we had corn, corn, corn. "When it's harvest time in peaceful valley!" I sang, making my sister laugh in the middle of the endless steamy weeks of shucking and stringing and snapping and shelling. Our hands felt raw.

But the corn wasn't good. We had saved seed corn from last year's crop instead of buying new seed; though the ears were as plentiful and full as before, the kernels were tough. I watched Benny Smallmon slow to look down from the county road at our huge corn patch and the pile of fresh-picked ears beside it, and heard his old red pickup rattle to a stop and whine into reverse as he backed down the driveway. We filled his truck bed, heaping the ears high in the center while he leaned his big belly over the fender and grinned. Benny lived on the old McRoberts place out at the breaks; his six skinny kids had dirt ground into their elbows and pale wispy hair clumping on their necks. They could use this corn even if it wasn't as sweet and tender as we had hoped.

As his truck pulled back up the driveway I looked over at Mom. "All that work," she said. "I'm so sorry. But even if it had been good corn—I just can't do it, honey. I thought I could let you sell it, but I can't."

"I know," I told her. My arms itched from the cornhusks. "He could have helped us load it, though, don't you think?" She saw my face and smiled back. Then she sobered. "Those poor little kids," she said.

>-|-◆>-•O-•◆-|-◄

A redtail hawk rises from the sage, circling higher and higher, and beyond the town in the valley below me are the Blues, their folded canyons mottled with gold and violet in afternoon shadow. Will Dean have his special fish soup waiting on the stove to welcome me home, the way he often does when I've been away? Trucks so far in the distance they look like toys wind their way up Cabbage Hill, heading for La Grande and Baker City and Ontario, maybe even Chicago. "Hot Dogs, Burritos, Ice Cream, Beer," says the first sign I can see from the freeway.

Only the privileged can afford to eat the way my family did when I was growing up—"organic" meats and fruits and vegetables, milk and eggs. Finding enough food of any kind is a problem for far too many people. Oregon—despite the cattle, sheep, and wheat ranches below these Blue Mountains and the rich farmland of western Oregon's famed Willamette Valley—has had trouble feeding its own residents: for three consecutive years, according to the people who measure these things, we were the nation's hungriest state. Dean and I fill the Boy Scouts' collection sacks with canned peaches, corn and green beans, sacks of bean soup mixes, boxes of instant pudding, oatmeal, rice. Our mail carrier leaves bags for us to set out by the curb, too. If there is message from the Food Bank in the stack of monthly bills, I seal another $25 check inside their small green envelope. I know it is not enough.

Food insecurity, it's called, the constant worry about where the next meal's coming from, the "uncertain ability to acquire acceptable foods in socially acceptable ways." So how would I describe what had I felt that night at the Blue Sky Restaurant? Food insecurity of a different kind? I pull off the freeway and turn up the hill toward our little house, a heaviness rising from my belly to settle in the center of my chest. Yes, I can still feel awkward or embarrassed when I'm eating—caught off guard by habanera peppers, say—embarrassed, but not ashamed. Shame is this weight I feel when, even for a moment, I forget what's important. What I have known since I was a child.

My family ate dinner in a restaurant for the first time the summer I was 21. We had been traveling all day—on our way home from a visit with Jill and her new husband—and my teenaged brothers had made short work of our sandwiches and apples by mid-morning. It was nearly dark when we slid gratefully into adjoining booths in a roadside café in Baker City. High desert cattle country. I had been paying my way through college with summer waitress work, so I was the family expert on hamburger steaks and French fries. "Bette, doesn't this taste especially good?" Mom asked over my shoulder. The woman who had stepped out from behind the counter to refill our coffee cups smiled, her face wearing the hours of her shift like a time clock. "You was just hungry," I heard her tell my mother.

Seeking Shelter

Most poor children feel ashamed of their homes. As adults, even if they have now earned college degrees, this feeling of shame spills over into the places where they currently live—at least, this was true of the people in a study by Donna Reed ("Overcoming the Silence of Generational Poverty" *Talking Points*, Nov/Dec. 2003). I look up from the computer screen where I've been reading Reed's research to glance around my own house: no, I can't honestly say that like 82% of the participants in her study, I am constantly trying to improve my surroundings. But there are other signs of kinship. When I turn the front doorknob on a blustery day, for instance—though I always feel grateful for this warm shelter and the aroma of bean soup coming from the kitchen—I find myself wondering *how safe am I in this place? Will this roof hold out the snow? How long will these walls stand against the wind?* What I'm really asking is, do I belong here? Can I stay?

Once I was evicted. The graduate student who had been coming over every evening that fall had fallen asleep on the couch with his red wool jacket zipped up to his chin, and as the room grew cold I covered him with a blanket and lay down beside him. The landlady, who lived just across the street, was aghast to find his car there in the morning: how could she subject her teenagers to such an example?

And once, the spring that tax levy failed and the school district cut my teaching position—also a surprise, and even more devastating than getting evicted—Dean and I had to sign a quitclaim deed to our house. Desperate to get out of our old trailer, we had bought when interest rates were high; now the country was in a recession; even finding a renter was out of the question. And we couldn't bring ourselves to miss a mortgage payment.

Later, when we were looking for another place to live, I picked out abandoned farmhouses as we traveled even though we were still miles from the town where I had found part time work. We could fix that one up, I kept thinking. One house was still painted blue but the roof was open to the sky, a lattice of charred two by fours. Against all logic, it called to me.

I too had stood in the snow watching a house burn, the biggest bonfire I had ever seen. Our mother had almost finished getting us dressed that morning when she smelled smoke and opened the stairway door to find flames already leaping across the upstairs walls—but Jill was missing one shoe, and Dad was the only one who still had a winter coat when we drove away.

Sometimes I wonder if it was hardest for my father, who had been born in that homestead log house. After all, it was the place he had always come home to. But Mom had already spent one cold spring living in a tent, after the "county house"—a shack down by the river loaned to Depression-era families who could not afford to pay rent—had flooded in the high runoff. I used to try to imagine it: being fourteen, unable to attend high school because my family had no money for textbooks, and then moving into a soggy canvas tent with six other people. "The worst part of it," she told me, "was that the tent flap faced the street." So maybe losing our house was even harder for her.

When a family burns out there is almost always a clothing donation box in the corner grocery and a money jar on the checkout counter. People come by with a couple of old kitchen chairs in the back of their pickup or a pot of baked beans on the passenger seat. My parents had lost everything—clothes, blankets, pots and pans. The kitchen table, their children's toys. Spoons and shoelaces. But the only help we received was a quilt made by the community women's club, with each woman's name embroidered on her square. I didn't understand. Years later, I learned that my father had told someone—maybe it was his initial shock after the fire, or it could have been the pull-up-your-own-bootstraps pride of the rural poor—that he didn't want any help.

How do we find shelter for our lives? The house that now stands on the old home place is a visible witness, a trail of bent nails and splinters, of one family's attempt to answer that question. It began as a two-room structure "just for now"—we would use it to house our chickens next year, or the year after that, Dad said. It had no foundation and no insulation. Constructed in a hurry after the fire with rough-cut boards rejected by the planer mill where my father loaded boxcars at night, it was a place for him to put us, his two little girls and the new baby, until there would be time and money to build a real house. But he would keep adding lean-to bedrooms for his growing family as the structure sprawled out from what he could never forget was a reject, rotten-lumber core. On good days it was something he could laugh about. We're living in a chicken house, kids. But it was hard for him to find humor in what had become a visible symbol of his failures. He sat at the kitchen table, hunched over his coffee cup, wishing aloud that this one would burn too. How can you add on to something that isn't true? he'd ask. Nothing in this place is level, or square. And this time they had insurance. This time there would be money to start over right. Or maybe they could set up a trailer, one of those new long ones that has everything you need built right in. One of these nights, during a lightning storm, he'd say, and my mother would turn back to the stove, her hands reaching for something she could not find.

The room where we all slept and dressed around the wood stove on cold winter mornings has been stretched into a space almost twice its size, but it is dark and windowless, since the bedrooms were added to its outside walls. The new section of living room has a big window but not much floor space, just a cramped circle around the island of the propane stove and its chimney. There's a bathroom now, and a washer and dryer out on the porch. Paint. Insulation in the ceiling if not the walls. The tar-paper tacked down with one by twos (*Does it come in any colors besides black, Dad?* Jill asked him once) has long since been replaced with battened board siding. But it's a hard house to live in, still.

Dean and I stayed there for those first few months after I lost my job. "One thing's certain, we can never move," I had joked, looking around our own garage. But only a few weeks later we would be driving pickup load after load down the Buford Grade and back up the Rattlesnake and trying to find room for our things in the house I had grown up in. We had sorted as carefully as we could in the shock of our sudden leaving, but later we would haul three loads of what we had carried with us back down the hill to the dump.

We spent the summer painting. Dean fixed the old wiring; we spread black sealant over the nail heads in the metal roof. But the radon meter we hung on the wall pointed to the danger zone, and I could never get the black-scuffed linoleum to feel clean. A previous renter's horses had chewed the outside windowsills. I scraped mold from the corners of the back bedrooms, thinking of my father's complaints about rotten lumber. Snow came early and deep, and I remembered how it had felt to be cold all winter. We had wrapped heat tape around the pipes, but would that be enough? The roof had to be shoveled and the shovels might knock loose the sealant; already there was a leak over the porch. Could that bulb keep the pump house from freezing at twenty below? We covered the windows with plastic that made us feel as if we were living in a cave but didn't do much to stop the currents of frigid air.

Houses hold memories, maybe even what people think of as ghosts. An old Montana farmhouse Dean and I had rented years before had one that had our dog growling into empty corners and both of us apologizing out loud for opening the attic trap door. As a child I had felt something I couldn't name at my best friend Barbara's house, too. Later I would learn that Clayton

Campbell, the navigator of Crew 13—the last of Doolittle's crews to bomb Tokyo Bay—had grown up in that house, and his young wife lived there with his parents while he was at war. The presence I could feel that winter in my own childhood home was my father, dead only since July. "This house is going to kill me," he had told me a few years before. He had been bracing himself against the back of the wooden rocker in front of the stove, trying to take a deep breath. His asthma and emphysema were getting worse. They had left the home place after he retired, following my mother's new job with the Corps of Engineers, but when she was 65 they had returned. I understood now why he would pull Mom along on his odyssey of campers and fifth wheel trailers, the apartments in Arizona and Lewiston, trying to find a safe place to live. Finally, they bought a bigger singlewide trailer near town. The trailer court was between the river and the timbered hillside, so they could still watch the whitetail deer crossing their yard in the evening dusk. He had been looking out that window, waiting for sunrise, moments before he died. "Don't get between me and the light," he said.

Of course, he could have borrowed money to build the real house he had always wanted—he would put it over there in the east field, he always said, where there would be no hill to climb through the snow to get out to the county road—but that would have meant mortgaging the land itself, and he just couldn't risk it.

➤—◦—O—◦—◄

My mother is standing in the kitchen doorway, looking down into the last cardboard box of things for the yard sale. "Oh, that little coffee pot you gave me," she says. A two-cup plug-in percolator. It had been part of a special understanding between us, I remember, a way of claiming something just the right size for her life. Had I given it to her when I was still in college? Or maybe when she moved to that small town in the Columbia Gorge, leaving Dad behind for those first few weeks as she found her own path to a new job in a new place. That was the fall she was "only 56," the same age I will be tomorrow. I can remember searching for such a coffee pot and the way we both laughed as I handed it to her. But I can't remember when. My mind is full of these moments now, thin-shelled ornaments hanging from invisible boughs. I stand up from the floor where I have been kneeling beside the box of spices—where to find room for the spices?—and wrap my arms around her. Gently, gently. Her spine is a fragile stem.

We are helping our mother move from the trailer parked near the river, where she has been living alone since our father died, back to the ranch. The house stands only a few yards away from the spot where the old homestead log house burned and where narcissus and daffodils still come up in the spring pasture. My sister has been living here for several years, her own health so precarious that we—my brothers and I, and the aunts who are still living—have been frantic every winter. What if she should fall? For the hundredth time I shake my head. But this is the way it's going to be, at least for now. There's a new assisted living facility in town, with patios that open onto the creek Mom loves, but she just wouldn't feel comfortable there, she says. Her clothes aren't good enough, or her furniture. Outside, the swallows are diving in noisy circles at the birdhouse, trying to reclaim it from the pair of bluebirds who got here first this year.

It isn't easy to push another life back into the old house. We have been sorting, packing and unpacking, moving as fast as we can. Everyone has to be on the road no later than two. Mom's things, Jill's things. Two toasters—which one shall we keep? We stumble through the accumulations of our own childhoods, our father, his parents. The aunts. No matter how many times we sort and haul away, no matter how much has been stolen by antique hunters or scavengers, there is always another rusty sickle blade or buck rake or remnant of stiff leather harness. "Grandma, how long has this place been here?" my twelve-year-old nephew wants to know. He's talking about the land itself. The earth. My mother reaches out to touch his face.

How can we rearrange my sister's things to make room for Mom's? We need a seating arrangement that is easy to walk through for people who both use canes. Let's move the bookcase, we finally decide. It's a major project, and it means sorting the books, deciding which ones we can put in the yard sale boxes. So here it is, my sister's life. The geology section. The law books. Double shelves of nutritional self-healing books. "That can go. That can go. No, I'm not ready to part with that." Astronomy, sociology, *Giants in the Earth*.

"I'm sorry," she says at last. "That's all I can do for now."

Driving home from the big moving weekend I am as exhausted as I have ever felt in my life, talking to myself just to stay awake, trying not to turn into a hawk on the curves between Dayton and Pomeroy and soar right off the highway toward the canyons of the Blues, so maybe what happens when I turn up Emigrant Avenue on the final stretch of my trip shouldn't surprise me. FREE WOOD. Big red letters spray-painted on the plywood fencing where the saddle shop burned last summer. I haven't seen a sign like that in years. Pendleton is as conservative as any other town in eastern Oregon, maybe more so, but somebody wants to free Wood. And I don't even know who he is. But the spirit hasn't died, and that's encouraging. FREE ANGELA DAVIS! spray-painted on walls, on sidewalks—and then I am laughing. They just want people to haul away the scrap lumber, of course. So they can start to rebuild.

I will need to make several more trips back to Idaho to finish unpacking the boxes still shoved into corners and to become a mapmaker to the house's inhabitants. (*We can't find the iron!*) And I am already thinking ahead to the coming moves.

Across the pasture from the house where Mom and Jill are living—they see it every morning as they sit down to breakfast, backlit by the sunset as they prepare supper—is the one room log cabin, still nestled under the big firs below the gate. Dad built it when he was seventeen. When my parents married, the cabin was not yet ready to move into: it was just log walls and an empty space for a window with a view across the pasture toward his own parents' homestead log house, and a roof with no stovepipe hole. For the time being, though, they were living in one of the little shacks assigned to the workers at Johnson's Mill. Dad had been a crosscut sawyer since his early teens—and he was a man now, 21—but they happened to need someone to sticker the lumber to let it dry, so that's what he was doing that first summer when the dye on the treated boards caused an infection that almost cost him his sight. Bill Johnson offered to hire them—or Mom, really—to cook in a spike camp. They went there and stayed overnight. But there was no lard or shortening, Mom said, only a big bucket of bacon drippings swarming with yellow jackets, and the place was an incredible mess. She went outside and threw up, and couldn't stop vomiting. They had to get back to town to the doctor. By that time she had decided she couldn't do it. She had only cooked for her brothers and sisters. She was eighteen years old.

Somehow they got gray building paper and rough-cut lumber to cover the cabin walls and Dad's father helped him cut a chimney hole, and then they stuffed the chinks between the logs with pieces of hand-split shingle and the whole family threw mud at the outside walls. "It sticks if you throw it," Mom said. Two years later, when Dad could see well enough to work part time, he was hired as a choker setter—the hardest job in the woods, and the most dangerous. He made $500 that year. "I kept a record of every penny," Mom tells me. "Every postage stamp!" They would live in the cabin for several more years. Jill lived there, too, as a baby, and it is where I was conceived.

"I was so young," Mom says of her days in the log cabin. "But I thought I was all grown up. I had been supporting myself for what seemed like a long time." She had been seeking her own shelter since she was fifteen, when she moved in with the doctor's family where she worked as a maid. "Irene, my good right hand," the doctor's wife called her. She cleaned and ironed and sometimes she wore a small white apron and cap: serve from the left, clear from the right. "I never know what she is thinking," one of the guests complained. Thoughts about pity, Mom tells me now, mixed with something like disdain.

But she slept in the same room with the family's daughter, and they were all kind to her until she fell in love with my father. Maybe the woman of that house thought about him the way she did about the neighborhood Indian child she had forbidden her daughter to play with. "He is a piece of yellow nothing," she said.

We are sitting at the kitchen table as she tells me this story; Jill has gone to town for something she needs. I want to get up and clear the counters, but everything needs to stay where it is so they can reach it without bending over. Sometimes my mother and I don't say anything for a long time, just glad to be together. It reminds her, Mom says at last, of a moment when she was four years old, drawing at another kitchen table while her mother worked. Her younger brother must have been napping and her sister was already in school. "Ain't we nice and quiet, Mama?" she said.

><+>-O-<+><

Location, location, location. In Pendleton, North Hill is the place to be, South Hill is not. The old gingerbread Victorians down on The Flats are divided into shabby apartments, but most people in that section of town live in houses much like the one I grew up in, the kind of houses that line both sides of the railroad tracks. Some of the older houses on the North Hill still have restrictive clauses to embarrass the real estate agents; for a long time the law to keep people of African ancestry off the North Hill unless they were on their way to a job as a domestic or a chauffeur was still on the books. Washington School, out by the river below the Pendleton Woolen Mill, is where most of the Indian children go. Their grandmothers were not allowed to use the public toilet at the courthouse in the early days. Tourists can take the Underground Tour to learn where the Chinese men lived; there's an opium den and a jail cell and what's left of a Chinese laundry. At first the Chinese had lived in small houses above ground, but they all burned to the ground one night. The only natural light in the Underground comes from the small squares of thick glass embedded in the sidewalk, the old fashioned kind I grew up walking over, wondering why they were there.

There are a few new low-income apartments in town now and an assisted living facility named for a tree that grows in the high desert, but most of the poorest people live in Sergeant City, run down barrack apartments built during World War II when Clayton Campbell was part of Doolittle's bomber crew training here. Rimming the skyline are the new houses that look like the box hotels in a Monopoly game. The new president of the college lives in one of these houses. It took men on bulldozers over a year to reshape the hill so the houses would have flat places to sit, and a road so the inhabitants could come back down when they wanted to. There aren't any trees.

Our little house is on the Southwest section of town, just high enough so that we can look between the houses to watch the lights of the trucks cresting Reith Ridge on their way down into the valley. This area used to be native grassland and then it was seeded to wheat, but after World War II it became Sherwood Addition. The street we live on has mostly two bedroom houses, and it is about as multicultural as Pendleton gets: young people with babies, widows, single men. Mexican families, and two white men with Asian wives. A Japanese family. One lesbian couple. And us. The street curves, so if I stand close to the kitchen window at night and look left, I can see the McDonald's arches.

When we walk our dog past Sherwood School in a half mile circle around our house, we pass two big storage shed businesses, and there are others all across town. Maybe people are trying to hang on to the pieces of their lives while they look for a safe place to live, or maybe the people in this town have so many things that they just don't have room for them all.

Just below those truck lights is the village of Reith. A sawmill and a tavern and lots of mud, and a whole lot of people living in houses that make the chicken coop I grew up in look like a home featured in *House Beautiful*. The valley below the mill is the first place to green up in the spring. When we drive the river road to watch the hawks that nest on the basalt cliffs, I think about Indians, how it must feel for the Cayuse and Umatilla people to look at this valley now.

I love our house. I wish it were in the mountains, or beside the Middle Fork of the Clearwater, or at least up on the prairie where we could watch the moon rise, but it is warm and light and just the right size for two people. Last summer we refinanced our mortgage so we could put on a new roof, gray shingles guaranteed to last longer than we will live. We put in new double-pane windows that open to let in the morning air, and a man came to install the kitchen exhaust fan we had been storing on a shelf for five years. There are blue blinds above my desk, and the little garage has a coat of white paint. Best of all, there's a gas fireplace. Our dog puts his front legs up on the hearth and lowers his chin to his paws and closes his eyes.

But our house is what the real estate people call a starter home, just right for a young couple and their first baby. You were supposed to keep trading up, someone explained to me recently. Increasing your value as you got older.

Once, when I was in junior high and especially vulnerable to such things, a boy sitting behind me on the school bus—a boy I wanted to like me—looked over my shoulder at a snapshot taken in my family's kitchen and said, before he thought, "Whose house is *that?*" The grease spots on the unpainted Celotex looked even worse in black and white. I'm not ashamed of the house where I live now, but when people come to visit, I sometimes regret that I have never bothered to learn the language of interior decorating. I don't really understand why none of that has seemed important to me. Good furniture and beautiful lamps were out of the question for so long that they still don't seem worth thinking about, I suppose. Or maybe I am just a slow learner. After thirty years we have finally acquired several places to sit, but the fabric of the couch is beginning to separate like strands on a broken loom. "We need to get that orange chair recovered," we say to each other. Buying art is another thing I have never learned to do. A friend has given me a half-dozen of her paintings, including a watercolor of the one-room cabin where my parents lived in those early years of their marriage, so I took down the yard sale print of the creek meandering under those big trees into a pasture. But we can't bring ourselves to let go of the girl leaning against her broom. I should frame my friend's watercolors—I should pay to get them framed, I mean—and hang them in better places, not just where there were already hooks in the walls. I'll do that, I keep thinking.

The best part about our house is the back yard. We have hung bird feeders outside the big window over the kitchen table, and when the goldfinches flash their spring colors against a background of pink—the crabapple tree blossoms in early April too—I can almost pretend that I live in the country again. Dean strings the hammock between the maple and crabapple, and we listen to the weaver finches coming and going from the birdhouse above our heads. The hammock was his gift for my 43rd birthday, just before I learned that I would lose my job and the view of Chief Joseph Mountain above our living room window. Chief Joseph, whose real name meant "thunder rolling from peak to peak" and who would not have named a mountain for himself, died in exile from the northeastern Oregon valley his people had called home for thousands of years, pushed out by others who wanted to build the kinds of houses they thought would keep them safe. Visiting children always want to climb in the hammock and be pushed, to tip it over and tumble out on the ground. They like to pick the grapes that trail over the fence from our neighbor's vines, the sweet seedless green kind, but they have to wait until summer is almost over, August and early September. We leave the hammock up until late October, like a porch swing quilted with yellow leaves. On clear nights we lie in it, cuddled together to keep from shivering, watching the stars.

Personal Hygiene

I have the kind of dry skin that makes my fingertips crack open, so I know it doesn't make sense to bathe so often. But after every T'ai Chi class my friend Susan and I head for the women's steam room, all that wonderful hot fog floating around us until my contacts threaten to swim out of my eyes, completely waterlogged. The steam room is not nearly as intense, either physically or spiritually, as the few Northwest Native sweat houses I have been invited to enter, but it's the closest thing available, and it's lovely. We have to take our dip in the women's Jacuzzi first. The water is not quite as hot as we wish and it would feel lukewarm, even cool, after a steam bath. The health club has adjusted the women's showers so almost no water comes out—I don't think the men would put up with this feeble trickle, and how women with long hair manage a shampoo I don't know—but Susan always saves the broken shower head, the real gusher, for me. Sometimes in late afternoon or evening if my shoulder muscles are a bit tight I fill the bathtub at home too. Soaking in Epsom salts, four cups in water deep enough to cover my shoulders, is a trick I learned from a massage therapist.

Once I was led through a very large house midway through its construction. The owners were the only employers in the one-mill town where I was teaching high school English, people who owned a team of polo ponies and later, a Thoroughbred that made headlines as Seattle Slew. Each child's bedroom would include a fireplace and personal sauna, my guide pointed out; but what I have never forgotten was the vertical Japanese immersion tub adjoining the master bedroom. Now she had my attention.

Cleanliness isn't really the point, just a happy byproduct. And although I prefer my water as hot as I can stand it, a snowmelt mountain lake will do too, and a river's current is even better.

My mother loves water too; so does my son. It's genetic, I tell myself. But of course I know the real source of my own desire for immersion: I grew up in a house without a bathroom.

Having an outhouse seemed fairly normal at the time. We called it the toilet; outhouse was the word my town friends used when they stayed overnight, the same ones who said things like, "You can't fool me—cows don't have horns!" Going outside to the toilet seemed as normal as going out to the barn or down to the well. Until I was eleven we carried all our water in buckets and of course had to heat both bath water and dishwater on the stove, so baths in the round metal washtub were fairly quick affairs in a couple of inches of water. Among my earliest memories is the wonderful feeling of Mama wrapping me in a towel and hurrying me, still warm, into flannel pajamas ("Dry me quick, Mama, before I chap and break in two!" Jill said once, making everyone laugh). When she had tucked us into bed Mama added another teakettle of boiling water to the tub for her own bath, and then it was Dad's turn. We weren't dirty enough to scare him, he said, but I thought being last was brave of him anyway. The electric range that replaced the old wood-burning cook stove when I was eight made baths a lot easier, especially on August nights, and then the summer after I turned eleven Dad dug a trench and piped the water into the kitchen. I could quit envying the old farmhouses with the pump handle right by the sink. Hot water just by turning on a faucet. He bought the biggest hot water tank that he could find, one with a quick recovery, and over four decades later it was still in service.

But we couldn't have a bathroom. The hand-dug well just wasn't strong enough to support all that flushing. Sometimes in late summer the well went dry in spite of our carefully measured water use and we were back to kettles simmering on the stove again, water from the barrels Dad filled in town. We had a longer metal tub now, though. Taking our baths in the kitchen—in full view of both doors leading outside, in a household of seven—meant that to ensure privacy bath time was restricted to evening. But it was mostly because we had to ration water so severely that we got the tub out only about once a week, washing our hair at the kitchen sink and doing washcloth-and-basin sponge baths before school every morning. Mom said I could take a bath in less water than anyone she ever knew: only about a half inch in the bottom of the tub. Dad worried aloud every night at the supper table about our failing water supply, and the difference between half an inch and an inch didn't seem all that significant.

Who didn't want a bathroom? It was out there in the future, one of those "someday" promises. But if it ever came true, we knew we would be giving up something, too. The stars, for one. Orion and Cassiopeia and the Pleiades, the big dipper, meteors that lit the top branches of the fir trees. The full moon climbing up from Huckleberry Butte. Deer over on the hill, red against June alfalfa, their white-flag surprise. Violet-green swallows swooping in, then lifting up just at the last minute. Would we come out here behind the house several times a day just to hear the red-winged blackbirds singing down at the pond?

By the early 1960s, many of our neighbors were drilling real wells and attaching bathrooms to their old farmhouses. All it took was money and a whole lot of faith. I would be almost through college before my dad could come up with either. After all, he had to repay the bank its $2000, nearly half his year's wages, whether the driller found water or not.

>−·◄≻·•O·•◄≻·◄

Sometimes I mention it in my community college classroom, if the discussion seems to prompt such a statement. "My family didn't have indoor plumbing." A strange expression, I think as it comes out of my mouth. What other kind could there be? And besides, we had the plumbing. What we didn't have was the toilet, the white enameled tub. The mirrored sink. A place to leave your toothbrush.

But I have to take a deep breath to say it—look some woman in the eye whose face tells me stories she can't bring herself to speak. The easy acceptance I felt as a child is hard to capture now. Things happened.

The first was unexpected. Dad's Aunt Nettie had always been just plain fun, and even after she draped her mink boa around my mother's shoulders—a string of thin, dry-eyed animals biting each other's tails, "You keep it until my next visit, Irene"—we all loved her. I knew about Nettie from the oldest stories, the ones my mother added details to on winter afternoons as I sat watching her fork press wheat designs into the pie crust, flecks of flour sifting like dust in the kitchen air and the radio on the shelf behind us tuned to KWSU. As a ten year old, Nettie had walked beside the wagon clear across the country with her younger sister, my grandmother Alice. She had wintered in the sod house in Sturgis and found her way to the farmer's barn by hanging onto the rope, and she had helped grub the service brush on her parents' Idaho homestead once the wagon finally got them here; just after her sixteenth birthday she married the man who had guided the family west in return for her hand. He was 40, and he drank.

Then Uncle Tommy had rescued Nettie and her little girl from that life, and all these years later, neither of them seemed quite able to believe their luck. Dad's face lit up, too, when he heard that Tom and Nettie were coming. I led the younger kids over behind the rock crusher where the tiny wild strawberries grew and we picked enough to make a quarter cup of wild strawberry jam for Nettie's light-as-air breakfast biscuits.

But when Nettie walked past the men who sat visiting in the shade of the walnut tree and saw the toilet, she turned and came back into the house. The reject lumber Dad had used last week when he replaced our old outhouse was greener than he realized and in this heat wave the boards had begun to shrink, twisting at their nailed-down edges to leave cracks between them. "I just don't know what to do!" Nettie told Mom. For the first time she seemed old. "It's all right," Mom said. "I'll take care of it." After she came back inside—she had tacked a sheet to the outhouse wall to cover the cracks—she went back to her dishes in silence. Nettie would return soon. Why didn't Mom say anything? "You'd think this was the first outdoor toilet your father's aunt had ever seen," she told me, finally. She looked at me, then, trying to smile. But something in her voice had changed. I picked up the damp dishtowel Nettie had been using and took a rinsed plate from Mom's hand, my fingers touching hers. What did it matter, now, that Dad had sanded the toilet seats so carefully, and made one child-sized?

When school started there were barn chores every morning, feeding and milking. I kicked off the stained buckle overshoes and left the wool jacket and jersey gloves on the back porch, washed at the kitchen sink and changed into school clothes. Skirts and dresses except on Fridays, now that we were in high school. Mom was just getting the younger kids out of bed while I helped make the lunches. "You girls need a bathroom," she said again. She said it the same way she had said we needed piano lessons, or a chance to be in Camp Fire. It would have been nice, all right. Trips outside on frosty mornings could be exhilarating, and winter was coming, the slip-slide icy trail. But I think Mom wanted it more than we did, and I couldn't for the life of me figure out why some of my town friends complained about not having two bathrooms. Our family's routines kept us clean, but there was no need for lingering, and taking turns was so automatic that it wasn't even conscious.

One morning the teachers announced that when the first bell rang the boys should go to class and the girls would meet in Study Hall, the old auditorium. They wouldn't say why. "Not the flower film again!" we said. "Maybe they think you need a refresher course," the boys kidded us. They were strangely excited.

When the bell rang our P. E. teacher leaned against the front of the stage, her arms folded across her chest. Someone, one of us, was dirty. Body Odor. It was so offensive that people had complained. Girls our age, Mrs. Hargrave said, need to bathe daily, and of course use underarm deodorant. What possible excuse could any of us have for not stepping into the shower every morning before school? It was humiliating to even have to say these things. We should know better, and now we did.

"No fair!" the boys said when we rejoined them in the band room. "You're not even going to tell us what it was about?" But nobody knew what to say.

The P. E. teacher had a degree from Mt. Holyoke. "What is she doing here?" Mom said when I slumped at my end of the kitchen table late that afternoon, my voice finding the words to talk about what had happened for the first time all day. "Think about it, Bette." Well, that's true, I thought. And I knew the one Mrs. Hargrave was talking about. Vicki Masterson, of course—and who could blame her if they'd ever seen the inside of the Masterson's house, and besides, she was trapped in that fat body and those awful old cotton house dresses and there wasn't a thing wrong with her mind, not a thing. But this teacher happened to dislike me—I wasn't sure why, but I knew it was so—and I couldn't help thinking she had really been talking about me. Why hadn't she just spoken to Vicki privately? My town friends had the same lingering question; I could see it in their eyes even as they had smoldered with indignation on the long walk to the classroom. Pam had put her hand on my shoulder.

It's in my hair, I thought the next morning, washing up at the kitchen sink. Even though I wear a hat, my head presses against the flank of the cow, and those damned goats I have to milk because the boys are so goddam allergic to everything on the goddam planet...and Dad saying how wonderful it is, all that extra milk making the pork chops so tender, and the chickens; all you have to have is a daughter, a built-in milkmaid, a filthy... I scrubbed until my skin felt raw. In some strange way I felt superior to Mrs. Hargrave. They couldn't pay me enough—all the rich bastards in the world put together couldn't pay me enough—to do what she had done. But I didn't feel clean.

>-+→-O-←+-<

One year at a time, people had advised me. Don't worry. By late May, though, I was getting scared. My 4-H cattle herd—two Hereford cows— had been sold to pay for my freshman year at the University of Idaho, but unless I could find a summer job I wouldn't be able to come back. And jobs for women were scarce in my hometown. When my aunt said I could get hired through a friend of a friend at a remote café on the Clearwater's Middle Fork—*131 miles from Missoula, 96 miles farther to Lewiston*, we told the tourists who emerged wide-eyed from the Lochsa canyon—I was saved. I would sleep in an upstairs room with the other two waitresses, in an old Forest Service cabin on the property, the owner explained. I'd work ten-hour shifts but she could only pay me for eight hours, and there would be no days off. The tub in the sunken cabin leaned crookedly against the wall, one corner four inches lower than the other; there was no glass or screen on the sleeping loft window, where mosquitoes and moths swarmed around the outside light. Back at the café, the owner took me into the men's restroom. "I don't want any of my hashers feeling like she's too good to clean a toilet," the woman said. Her pink uniform was torn at the shoulder. "Get down on your hands and knees; I don't want just the top to look good. I want it cleaned." Something was pounding hard against my rib cage. Without this job there would be no more literature, no more history classes...probably there were specific things everyone did when they cleaned a toilet. Procedures. I got down on my knees and made it up as she stood there watching.

But I am intimately acquainted with the rituals of toilet scrubbing now—sinks too, and tubs. So I am as startled as everyone else at the words that come out of my mouth. "My bathroom isn't big enough," I hear myself saying. The out of town members of our writers' group are coming to spend the night with us, looking forward to getting better acquainted with us in our rural setting. "There's no room for guest towels, not even a place to put an extra roll of toilet paper!"

"I know what you mean," a younger woman says into the silence. But how can she? I don't even know what I mean. True, our house was built in 1948, when post-war builders understood the necessities: sink, tub, and toilet. Sitting on ours is a bit of a squeeze for a wide-shouldered person wedged between the basin and the door. We barely found room to add the mirrored medicine box above the sink when we moved in a few years ago. Just outside the bathroom door are drawers and shelves; if you need something, all you have to have is an intimate relationship with the occupants of the living room. Or learn to think ahead.

Why am I still embarrassed about such things?

But the youngest member of our group is worried, too. The visiting writers have won major awards. They are Real Writers. Her own guest, she says, will have a toilet and sink, but will have to trek upstairs and through her kitchen to take a shower.

Back at my computer that evening, I e-mail the visitors to offer my twin bed. As it happens, though, the bed isn't claimed and I have a wonderful time sharing poetry and pizza in someone else's living room. "At least I have a bathroom," I will tell my friends when we meet again. "I don't know what gets into me sometimes." That evening, like a sheepherder lying back onto her wagon bunk at the end of a long day, I sink shoulder-deep into water so warm it's nearly hot. The previous owner of this house, another teacher, has left exotic maroon-striped wallpaper—and strangely enough, I have come to like it, even though it is starting to ease loose where it joins the ceiling. In a catalog called "Make Life Easier" I have stumbled upon something called ZAP! which promised to remove decades-old brown stains from porcelain tubs when everything else has failed. The tub shines.

Is it the war news leaking in through the bathroom door—left ajar, as always; I can't seem to get used to closing it—that makes me remember Mr. Forester? He taught U.S. History, briefly, until the end of September when the National Guard unit from our town was called up to prepare for possible service in a southeast Asian country I didn't remember studying in fourth grade geography. Laos? A lot was still ahead of us in 1961, and we had a sense of it that morning. I'd had to run, my instrument case bumping against my leg, to make the morning farewell ceremony around the flag pole: they needed those trumpet calls on *The Star Spangled Banner*. Mr. Forester had looked so different in his uniform.

I add more hot water, turning the tap with my foot. Mr. Forester, I remember, had told the U.S. History class a story late one afternoon about a friend of his who had moved into a small trailer and lived by himself while he finished high school. There was no running water so the boy had to take daily sponge baths. He heated the water on the small propane stove. Maybe it was the Quonset-hut classroom full of sweating, self-conscious teenagers that made Mr. Forester bring up the subject. He had looked pretty hot and miserable himself in that long-sleeved white shirt and tie. Or maybe he had heard about the personal hygiene lecture and wanted to leave us with a different message before he took himself off to be shot at. "There's more than one way to be clean," he said.

High school. Surviving it isn't easy, even now. The tub is slippery-clean, zapped into ageless beauty. A dowager empress without her wrinkles, like the women on the Oil of Olay ads. Would I have discovered makeup if I had grown up in a house with a roomy bathroom, plenty of space on the counter for eye shadow and mascara? Not likely. After all, lack of opportunity was only part of it. "If you don't like my face, look somewhere else," said a young Ralph Nader—this was in the days when he wore work boots with his suits—and I knew I had a kindred spirit even if he was male and not really expected to "put his face on" before going out the door every morning. But it did take me a while to give up scented deodorant. All of us were quite religious about its use in our high school days; it may even have been that year's deodorant-of-choice, men's Right Guard spray, that Mrs. Hargrave found so offensive. "In the mature male," the muted-with-horror voice on the TV commercial had told us as the camera revolved around Greek statues, the broken stumps of their arms lifted just enough to reveal gray-shadowed armpits—"and in the mature female..." Glands. Our bodies were, we already knew, not just suspect but guilty; we all dreaded the days when we had to carry an extra sanitary napkin in our brown lunch bags and worry that the clock hands had actually frozen this time on their imperceptible crawl toward noon. Was it any wonder that our bodies were betraying us again? Warnings were everywhere: halitosis, dandruff, ring around the collar. Even smoking might help. "You take a puff, it's springtime."

Hygiene. From Hygieia, the daughter of Asclepius—that's her sacred snake entwined on the Father of Medicine's healing staff. The goddess of Health.

What does it really mean, I wonder, to be healthy? To have a personal relationship with Hygieia? We gather in health clubs now to ponder that ongoing question—the shallow childhood catechisms of toilet and deodorant long behind us—still spinning and stepping to the beat of our own blaring hymns. Hygieia's svelter acolytes converge on our club at 5 p.m., dressed for mating prospects as well as cardiovascular challenges. But my early morning locker room colleagues are mostly harried teachers rushing off to work with their sweat-dampened T-shirts stuffed in their gym bags and the over-sixty Aquatics for Arthritics crowd, women who have long since accepted the evolving shapes of the self. In the T'ai Chi class, too, there are all sorts of bodies—thin, tall, short and round. Muscular. For T'ai Chi, I reflect, they all seem to work equally well. *Breathe into the dan t'ien. Move from the center.*

I stretch a foot up to add hot water. Five more minutes.

A Place to Sleep

There aren't enough beds in this new house, so Jill and I get to sleep with Mama. Daddy sleeps on the scratchy black cot at the foot of the bed. It's hard to climb up on because it humps up in the middle. Cold air blows through a crack below the window—it's really more like a shed than a house—but if I stand here on the humpiest part, I can look out across the snow to where our real house used to be. All that's left is a black circle in the middle of all this white, chunks of charred logs jutting up from the snow. Our beds burned up too.

When we move to town so Jill can start first grade, she and I sleep on something called a davenport. It rolls us into the middle—toward the crease where it folds—but even with the electric sheet under us and the flannel one Mama has held against the stovepipe on top of us, and the wool blankets over that, it's freezing cold so we don't mind. We press together like spoons. Mama and Daddy's bed is right next to us because there is only one room in this little house. Our new baby brother's small blue crib just fits but when Mama reaches over to rock it in the night the crib scratches a line down to bare metal across the refrigerator door. It's 24 below zero. We have to keep the baby warm, Mama says. Dad sleeps with one foot out, ready for anything. Jill's against the wall and I'm on the outside. I wriggle one foot sideways and out into the air but it's way too cold and I jerk it back in again. We're wearing our pajamas and our bathrobes and long brown stockings with garter belts. Garters bite when you roll over on them, but we try not to move because then we'll have to start over to make a warm place. In the middle of the night the lumpy wires in the electric sheet turn into snakes, big ones, little ones, all writhing toward me like long balloons. When I wake up screaming I am in my mother's arms. "Bud, you've got to quit scaring them with rattlesnake stories," she scolds. Dad is watching from the bed, looking sad. One snake is still wrapped around me but it's just my baby ring after all and Mama pulls it off my finger and puts it into her small cedar box, and after that the snakes don't come back.

Dad has been building us another house in the middle of the alfalfa field, right next to the pile of ashes. He says it will be a chicken house someday. I try to imagine Rhode Island Reds and White Leghorns in the living room where we sleep, Jill and I on a rollaway and Tommy in a full sized crib next to Mom and Dad's bed. This house has a kitchen too. We have to be very quiet because Dad goes to work at night so when we wake up he has just gone to sleep. All night long, while we have been sleeping, he has been loading stacks of heavy boards into boxcars. I wonder if it's dark inside the boxcars. Does he get scared? We stand close to the bed. "I think he's awake," we whisper. "I saw his eyelid move." A flicker, there, just at the corner of his mouth. Yes! He's trying not to smile! He's awake!

When we move back to town (because now I'm six and Jill's in third grade and there's still no school bus) we live in the duplex next to Aunt Edie and our favorite cousins. Jill and I sleep in the bedroom in the only bed and Dad and Mama sleep on another davenport. This one is purplish-red and there's a place that pokes you when you sit down. Tommy's crib is along the kitchen wall. He can climb out of it now and once Aunt Edie takes a picture of him crawling through the hole in the screen door into her side of the house. The bedroom doesn't have any windows but Mama reads us a chapter of the Bobsey Twins every night and I can never stay awake to hear the end and learn what happened to Freddie and Flossie. I hope no one ever starts calling me Flossie. Why are girls' names so silly? Nan is better than Flossie, but Bert is the best. Bette and Bert sound almost alike, though. And then I am asleep, because going to school makes you very tired, Mama says. She says that's why Jill and I need the bed more than grownups do.

>─┤◆>─●─<◆┤─<

Not long ago I heard a story on National Public Radio about a man about my own age, someone easily mistaken for a college professor, who has been homeless for six years. Occasionally, he said, he gets jobs house-sitting for friends. The hardest part comes in the last few nights as he counts down the hours he can spend in a real bed. A comfortable place to lay his body. Do the sociologists have it all wrong, I wondered? Maybe the simplest way to decide what social class we belong to is to forget all those questions about money and education and position and power and ask ourselves, "How much time do I spend thinking about where I will sleep?" I remembered the Chinese calligraphy teacher in Mark Salzman's book *Iron and Silk* —when Salzman asks him what two things he thinks about most, the teacher says, "Eating and sleeping." He is amazed that young Salzman, a recent Yale graduate who has come to China to teach English and to study martial arts, thinks most about being liked, especially by women, and about mastering something well enough to earn recognition for it. "But these goals can be achieved so easily!" he says. "All you have to do is be kind and work hard. But to eat and sleep well, that is a difficult wish, because you cannot control these things yourself."

I think about that calligraphy teacher in the middle of the night when I'm trying to sleep.

Everyone's sleep pattern breaks in the night, usually about every two hours, the doctor has told me. But most people rise to the surface and sink back into the liquid depths without coming to full consciousness. They don't jerk awake, alert and ready. They can't tell exactly what time it is, recognizing the pre-dawn hours like turns in a familiar path: 12:50, 2:15, 3:35. If by chance a technician were to attach wires and electrodes to their temples in a Sleep Center, they would quite obligingly sleep—for a period of time long enough to be measured. Yes, he says, these pills are addictive. He takes them himself. Humans have to sleep.

Sometimes my aunt Carolyn has trouble sleeping too. When I visit my mother, who has decided to move into an assisted living apartment in Lewiston, I stay at Carolyn's house. "Did you get any sleep?" Carolyn asks every morning, her eyebrows lifting exactly like my mother's do when she's worried. If Mom weren't ten years older than Carolyn they would have been mistaken for twins. Did their mother's forehead wrinkle like that too, I wonder?

Two weeks before Carolyn's fifteenth birthday and a year before I was born, this grandmother I would never meet jumped from the bridge into the January current of the Clearwater River. "When they pulled Emily out on the other side, there by the cemetery," a distant relative had told me once, "she may have still been alive. I can't remember."

"Your mother was a mother to me, too," Aunt Carolyn says when Jill and I try to thank her now for driving Mom to another doctor's appointment, or to the college jazz concert or her physical therapy. For dropping by her small apartment nearly every day. It's as if our mother has three daughters, not two. What was it like, I had wondered when I was a child watching Mom and Aunt Carolyn walking out to the garden together, those twin shapes silhouetted against the afternoon sun, to have a sister ten years older than you, or ten years younger? "Carolyn was such a beautiful child," Mom had always said. "Everybody loved her." Before she was married—when she was still dating my father—Mom would climb into the bed she shared with this eight-year-old sister and whisper the secrets of her grownup evening, how she and Bud had walked all around the dark streets hand in hand, singing "Winter Wonderland."

"She gave me the only mothering I had," Carolyn tries to explain. Of course, of course. By the time this youngest child was born, Emily's depression had deepened.

So when Carolyn came up the mountain to the little one room log cabin where my parents were living, Mom simply slid closer to Dad to made room for her sister in the bed. After their mother died, Carolyn rode the bus to the Bremerton shipyards where she could live with another sister and help with a new baby, and go to high school. When she came back in her sixteenth summer, her father had remarried. "That summer was such a hard time for your folks," Carolyn said. I can only imagine. The war in Europe had just ended and my recently drafted thirty-year-old father had been sent home just before he would have finished boot camp; Jill was a toddler and I was a newborn. They were living in that tiny duplex, and they had almost no money. "It can't have been easy for them to take me in. But they made a little cot for me on the back porch."

Is this what it comes down to? Does the confidence to walk freely under the sun grow out of knowing that you have a place to sleep when night returns? My grandmother Emily, I know from the fragments of stories spoken around kitchen tables, had never been quite sure of her place. Where did she belong? Her birth certificate declared her *illegitimate*. When she was sixteen, Emily had ridden the train from Prince Edward Island to Idaho to find her mother, but her mother was not happy to see her. "This is my sister," she told her neighbors. She put this daughter to work, though, eight years of cooking and washing and cleaning and making beds for the boarders in her hotel. Eventually Emily married and had her own children, but her husband yearned for someone not so sad. She did have physical shelter—a roof, if only a tent roof that spring of the flood...but did she have a safe place to face the darkness?

Aunt Carolyn and I had spread a blue and pink flowered coverlet over my mother's new bed, our hands resting a moment at the corners to tuck in the soft Grandmother Spider-pattern Pendleton blanket. We had found a blue loveseat, a new blue chair. And a princess daybed, white with tiny pink roses. "I want her to have nice things, things of her own. A *girl's* room," Carolyn had said when we helped my mother settle into her assisted living apartment. "She's never had one before."

My mother had a bed she could call her own only once when she was a girl, and briefly—the year she got to return to high school because that summer she had landed a Depression-era job in the hospital kitchen as a Tray Girl; finally she could buy her textbooks. Before that, during the winter of what should have been her freshman year, she had slept in the sunken hole of a broken-spring couch while her three brothers kicked and groaned and shivered under their blanket on the only bed. "Shove over, you crazy nut!" she could hear them complaining. On those summer mornings she walked to the hospital at 5 a.m., and at 11, after breakfast was prepared and she had hauled it up hand over hand on the dumb-waiter and the thick, heavy crockery had been retrieved and washed, if she'd had time to set up the trays again for the noon meal, the cook often said, "Why don't you go lie down on my bed for an hour?" The cook had a room in the hospital—a bed and night stand; so did the laundress and the janitor. Yes, all three had children, Mom had explained when I asked, but the job was seven days a week and the beds were part of their pay since they had to live at the hospital. One sent her children to live with her sister, the other paid a woman to care for them. The janitor's wife and two boys lived here in town and he could go home for dinner sometimes, but he too had to be close because accidents might come in, a young sawyer or choker-setter too badly mangled to manage the stairs and the janitor would be needed to pull the elevator rope, a weight even heavier than the dumb-waiter loaded with six trays. *I'd never had cramps before, but that summer I was just sick with them, and the cook knew… It would be child abuse now,* my mother had mused. *Imagine a doctor letting a young girl do such work! He's the one who got me the job, of course; a favor—jobs were so hard to come by.*

"When did you get to go home, Mom?" I had asked her.

"When the work was done. Oh, I guess usually about nine. The cook and the laundress were both so good to me. The janitor was too. I can still hear the nurse calling him. *Benson! Benson!* Another dirty job to clean up."

⪼⫶⟡⫶⪻

Home again, I slip under the comforter and back into Dean's arms. All night we will roll together, turning first his way and then mine in a queen-size bed, my foot snaking out into the air sometimes just like my father's did, a woman finally warm enough, finally too warm. I've long since shed the blue sleeping shirt. But I turn again, pull his arm around me until his hand touches my breast. "Mmm," he says softly. He doesn't wake. We float in a deep green pool between stretches of whitewater.

Thirty years ago we carried a mattress on the top of a blue Ford Falcon, each of us reaching a hand up to hold it on. We had a washed-out sleeping bag with a broken zipper and one pillow, and now we had a five-dollar mattress. Things were beginning to look up.

By fall I had found a teaching job and we bought a new mattress to put on the floor—the cheapest one in the Sears catalog, four inches of soft foam. And we had a new neighbor, a wiry Montana horsewoman named

Blondie. We had met her just after we had finished carrying all the books, *Moby Dick* and *English and Scottish Ballads* and *House Made of Dawn* and Shakespeare and Chaucer and *The Scarlet Letter*, box after box, from the U-haul cartop carrier into this rented farmhouse at the base of the Mission Mountains. Blondie had lived in the house before the owners came out from Chicago to renovate it, she said; now she would be batching in the cabin, a low-slung gray building that looked more like a shed over there across the pasture. The barn was still hers to use, though, and the outbuildings. She raised Tennessee Walkers. Not enough people around here knew enough about horseflesh to appreciate them, which was too bad.

Sure enough, someone came out and hooked a tractor to the rough-board shack and pulled it over behind the farmhouse where she could plug in a ceiling light and where her pickup tires could find the purchase of the long, rutted driveway when the deep snows hit. To our mid-twenties eyes Blondie was a phenomenon. Already we had seen her ride the buck out of a kid-spoiled gelding—sharp glacial field rocks scattered all around this impromptu rodeo, and an abandoned spike-toothed harrow nearly beneath it—and she had asked me to help her pull a colt, saving both him and the birthing mare. Sixty-five, and still tougher than whang-leather.

One night when we knocked on her door to deliver a phone message she invited us in. Sliced raw potatoes sizzled in a cast iron fry pan on the small pot-bellied wood stove, but what I saw first was the bed. Just a double bed, but it took up most of the house. Metal bedstead, gray and brown patchwork quilt. Made from old wool coats, I thought—like the one I used to sleep under, grateful for its weight on below-zero nights. One straight-backed wooden chair in the corner. There was no room for a table.

Our faces reddened on the stove side but freezing air pushed through the cracks behind us and we stood with our hands shoved into our coat pockets while Blondie told us a story. "That ten mile road out to the main highway? Used to be named for the Kootenai family that lived in this cabin years ago," Blondie said. "Then the County changed it to Hearns Road. They had money, the Hearns. Big dairy farm. Just off the highway; the Andersons live there now. During the Depression when people got desperate, they would come with empty jugs, ask for just enough milk for the babies." And Hearns would give it to them, she continued. But with a lecture. *You folks oughta get yourselves a cow.* I could almost see them standing there, waiting, no money to pay with, their hands empty at their sides.

"Finally," said Blondie, "it was just too much, and one day they had a parade. Right past the courthouse and down Main Street. Twenty or thirty people who had no hope of getting a cow, with a big sign: HEARNS' COW GIVES MORE MILK THAN OURS."

Could Blondie still be alive, I wonder, still claiming her place in the world? I push back the comforter, folding it over Dean's shoulders; it's the same gray-blue comforter that was on my parents' bed. They took it camping too, sleeping in the back of the little green Datsun pickup by the river. On the last day of his life I sat with my father wishing he could sleep, but there was no escape from his pain. He pulled himself up and looked at me, his eyes saying everything he could not. I close my own eyes, open them again. Our bedroom ceiling is lit by this month's full moon pushing through layers of winter clouds. Ghosts of memory drift across it, old negatives linked frame after frame into motion. This time I'm tossing that pink rubber ball into the back of the old pickup—that '37 Plymouth?—as we pack to move to the one-room house in town. I want to make sure the ball comes with us. My father sets the chest of drawers against the cab and takes a step backward onto the ball. "Sonofabitch!" He picks it up and throws it hard. It bounces off the roof and out into the field grass. Mom pulls me back inside and takes a book from the top of a still-open box. I know all the words by heart— *Moving day, moving day. All my toys are going away!*—but she reads it to me anyway, her arm curving around me to turn the pages. *I wondered where I would sleep tonight, but when my bed came in, I was all right.*

"An off-the-floor bed!" When my own son was four he was primed for adventure. There was not enough room in his little walk-though trailer bedroom for both a twin bed and his toys, so Dean bought two-by-fours and built a single bunk with a red and blue ladder and side-rails, and a place for Tonka trucks and Lincoln Logs underneath. Wearing a red plastic fire-hat and a yellow oxygen tank over his fuzzy pajamas, Josh rescued Baxter the teddy bear over and over, hauling him up with a length of clothesline from an imaginary ledge far below. And he leaped from the bunk, launching his little body all the way through the doorway into the living room. "I'm practicing, Mom," he explained. "I need to learn how to fly."

Moonlight. Or is that first light now? I close my eyes, but tonight, I can tell, is not one for sleep. Did Emily lie awake in the darkness too, I wonder? I began to have difficulty getting to sleep about the time I learned how my grandmother had died. "Sleep knits up the raveled sleave of care," Mom told me on those nights, sitting on the edge of my twin bed to touch my forehead. By then our parents had cashed in our $25 savings bonds, Jill's and mine, and bought us twin mattresses and box springs. We still shared a lean-to bedroom—the chicken house in the alfalfa field had sprouted three tiny rooms along its east and south sides as two more babies had arrived. Jill played the radio as low as it would go, but Dad, who had to get up at 4 a.m. now that he was on day shift at the planer mill, wanted everyone in bed by nine and that damned thing *off*. Sometimes in the night I'd hear him making coffee, pulling out his chair at the end of the table. Coffee helped him sleep, he said. Other times, in the midnight silence, I could hear my sister crying. I wanted to climb out of bed and cross the cold floor and crawl in beside her, let's be spoons, but the one time I had whispered, "Jill?" she had simply swallowed her sobs, pretended I had heard nothing. I tried not to breathe.

Then, for several long weeks, I slept hard. I couldn't wake up. Barn chores, supper and homework, bed. "Don't you want to watch Dobie Gillis with us? It's only eight o'clock, honey..." Nmmmph. When Mom called softly at six, time to get up, I thought about the sickbed at school. If I could only get out to the barn, then into my clothes and onto the school bus, I could go lie down. Fall full length onto it. Sleep all day. Still in a fog, I pulled on the black-checkered mackinaw on the back porch, left the buckle overshoes flapping. Winter air braced me on the lead-stumble walk to the barn. By the time I'd stepped off the bus onto the school sidewalk, I knew I could keep going, class to class; no, you can't really go to the sickroom, I told myself, but it's sixth period and you'll be home soon, in bed—

Insomnia, I know, is just the flip side of this kind of sleep. Heads, tails. But it's easier on this side. Sometimes I even embrace these night hours like an old friend. Back at the home place, I know, Jill is asleep in the same bedroom our parents once shared, switching on the radio when she wakes in the night. Dean rolls over and this time I turn the other way, reach for my watch and pull it under the covers where it lights my private tent with its green glow. 3:45. I'll get up, maybe do some writing before the early morning T'ai Chi class. I shut the bedroom door behind me gently.

"Your house would fit inside my garage!" a woman once told me. Still, who needs more than this? Two bedrooms: one for sleeping, one for writing. And jammed into the corner between the desk and the file cabinet is a second small bed—for visiting friends, or poets; for children, for people of any age who are weary to desperation, about to fold. Anyone who needs a place to lie down, a place to sleep.

Constellations

The woman at the desk nearest mine left school long ago, and she is not sure she can write well enough to pass this class. "I'll be 50 when I get my degree," she says. "I'm 50 now," I tell her. We look at each other. Her left eye has the same slight tic mine gets sometimes when I am exhausted.

Her first essay begins under water. There are two girls in the tub, she writes. One lies on the bottom, a shadow; dark hair floats up at the edges of her vision. The other girl can still feel the step-father's hands around her throat, and the icy water gushing from the faucet. A light bulb dangles from a cord above the tub, a bright blur beyond the water. She is still alive, she knows, as long as she can see that light.

"Is it too much?" she asks. "Maybe it's not appropriate for a college writing class." Her gaze is steady.

She is a "non-traditional student." Like at least half of the members of this class—people from 15 to 77 who have driven up the hill for their first day of community college. Home-schoolers and dropouts, protégés; displaced loggers and single mothers; mill-hands and cannery workers and assembly line production workers with scarred knuckles and elbows and knees, aching backs. They sit next to the eighteen-year-olds just out of high school. What everyone has in common on the first day of Writing 121 is feeling a little scared. They know what's coming, or think they do.

But I am buoyed with September hope. "Forget everything you've been told about writing," I have told them—"unless you've been lucky enough to meet a teacher who didn't own a red pen." They looked at me. "I'm speaking metaphorically," I tried to reassure them. "Red pens can blaze as well as slash. You can write in any color you choose. We're here to learn to be more fully human. Don't write to tell people what you know, write to discover something you didn't know you knew. Be honest."

Every fall I think Freshman Composition will save them.

"You get to make your own constellations," I tell the woman who kept herself alive in that bathtub. "Remember those night stands that James McConkey saw all over the sky? Or Ursa Major—some people see a bear, some a dipper." I am so excited about her next essay—"Education"—that I see it as a new image: a skyful of stars, her pencil connecting, weaving four dimensions. "You have so many experiences, so many stars," I say. *For ten years*, she has written, *I lived on the street.* "And this part—it's somewhere in your notes—yes, here: about your grandmother burning her manuscript in the oven as her baby daughter watches. The husband's disapproval of her writing...be sure to get that scene in, somehow, in the final draft." I pause, read some more. "The trick is finding the patterns." She nods.

"My teacher says I have too many stars," I read in her next revision. I find it pushed under my door with a yellow sheet torn from a legal pad: "I'm sorry I can't make it to class. My fever's too high; I have to go home."

For a week I watch Orion sliding down the pre-dawn sky. I find him, always, in the same place, just above the bare top branch of the smallest maple tree. I stand in the yard, shivering; sometimes even when I close my eyes I seem to see meteors streaking across the blackness. *Will her life really be any different because of this class?* My breath is a white cloud against the moon. Like my words: pencil-ashes drifting in the margins of my students' papers.

It's traditional to think of teaching the writing courses as a hateful chore best left to graduate students or teaching assistants. Or as the curse of the community college teacher—who is offered no such luxuries, and five classes to boot. We lug papers home every night of the week, squinting at our desks or kitchen tables until it's time to go to bed, past time. Heavy book bags, and muscles spasms, always, just above our shoulder blades. But Writing 121 is the one class every student must take. And by state rule, the course must relate to the humanities. So it's our chance, and theirs.

>-I-◆→-O-←◆-I-<

"Retention," the dean tells us. "It's in your own best interest." We look across the table at her. Although our writing classes have waiting lists during the two-week period when students can still begin a new class, by mid-term— the fourth week class list is the one that counts for state funding—some of the desks are empty. "When numbers get serious," I hear Paul Simon singing inside my head, "they leave their mark everywhere..."

We have arranged this meeting to ask that the college replace the teacher who retired last fall. If our courses were less crowded, if we had more one-on-one time with each writer... Instead, the dean is threatening more cuts.

"Visit with your students," she says. "When I was teaching, I didn't just sign a drop slip. I talked to students, asked why they were dropping. Sometimes they didn't know about peer tutoring, for example. I offered alternatives." She smiles. "Sometimes they just need a personal touch, a bit of encouragement. Get to know them."

My friend Katharine stares at her. I close my eyes, but I feel a hand on my shoulder. It's the oldest member of our department, a man who has been teaching for forty years.

Back in my office, I touch my new stack of papers gently. A few hours after my father's funeral, James Baldwin had written, *a race riot broke out in Harlem. On the morning of the 3rd of August, we drove my father to the graveyard through a wilderness of smashed plate glass.* What connections can you find, I had asked my students, between public events and what's happening in your own lives?

What they have told me, though, was what Baldwin had told them: for them, fathers were the public events. Sara's father had gone to prison after his third drunk driving arrest, and for three years, she wrote, life was good. Joe had sat in front of the evening television with his dad, both of them still carrying a light coating of sawdust in their beards and under their nails, the day Joe's friend Chuck lost his fingers—just before quarter-time—at the sawmill. Linda's father hadn't spoken to her for seventeen years. Allison's father, a fundamentalist minister, had died of AIDS. *I'm the next version of my father,* wrote Philip. *Whether I like it or not.* "Every night my dad lay on the floor with the heating pad under his back," Isaac told me. "'What did you learn in school today, Son?'" Some of the fathers had come home at night and tossed their children in the air, or held surprises behind their backs, Barbie's and cool CD's; then they didn't come home any more. "I had only seen him drink once before—one beer, at a Fourth of July picnic." "My mother dug a hole under the apple tree, and we buried his picture," Sheila wrote. "I knew he wasn't really dead, but I knew he was gone." "At first it was fun," Steve said, "sitting for hours in the boat on the Snake River, talking about everything and nothing, casting out into the water. But after I started playing ball, we weren't close any more. He didn't like baseball. At his funeral last summer, all people talked about was how he much he loved fishing."

"I never thought I could be no writer," Eddie calls down the hall. His first effort is only a paragraph long, but in that half page he's been stabbed four times. He sounds elated. Or maybe he just wants me to think he is. With Eddie, I am still not sure. "Use your own language, tell your own story," I have told him, leading him, word by word, across the page. "Trust us to hear you." What is it like to lie face down on a gurney in a crowded Los Angeles emergency room and feel your life lifting above you?

"You people can't understand, though," Eddie says. "It's so different here."

Can we imagine what it's like to be eighteen and have cancer, a rare and deadly kind that grows on the face? Katie wonders. Jeremy describes waking up in the hospital, his own face still bloody; he cannot remember words or numbers or people's names. "School used to be easy," he writes. "Now C's come hard." Kyonghui writes about leaving her mother behind in Korea. Laura shares a haunting dream: she has to visit her mother in jail. Her husband, a corrections officer at the prison, holds her in his arms for the rest of the night, but she can't go back to sleep. Mary hears her foster daughter upstairs packing a suitcase. Paul remembers being on guard duty and oil wells burning against the darkness. Ben has been so quiet. "I lie awake in the dark and ask myself: am I a racist?" he writes.

Steve hasn't been to class, and there's a message asking me to return his call. "I didn't realize until I wrote that paper that my dad was too old to play baseball with me," Steve says. "It opened up some things... I had to come home and straighten some things out." Teresa may not make it, either. "Years ago—back in junior high—a teacher asked me to show the new girl around, make her feel at home," she has written. "Joanna and I became friends, but because she is black, my grandfather disinherited me." Now, midway through the term, her grandmother has died, and the grandfather has called to remind the family that Teresa isn't welcome at the funeral. Ma Ling comes to see me, a drop slip in her hand. "In China, my brother was everything," she said. "Here, he's nothing. His wife says she is in love with another Chinese student at the university. I am unable to think." "Addiction affects not only the user, but the entire family," writes Maria. It is her last paper; we will never see her again.

When the woman returns, still pale, she has a stack of yellow notebook paper, her words climbing across the pages at a sickbed angle. I watch as the grandmother feeds her own life story to the kitchen cookstove, page by page, while a baby daughter watches from the highchair. Then a girl just past puberty spends the summer in jail, juvenile detention the price of her flight to survival. How to find a place to sleep on a winter street? Scene after scene. Where will she take me? I finger the bottom corner of each page, eager for the next. *And now, college—an advanced degree, a profession, "social" work—are these light and air, food for some deep hunger, or are they just more ways of defining the limits, of telling me who I am and who I cannot be?* she asks.

The term is nearly over when I find myself thinking about Mike. He left school three years ago, but his papers still echo in my mind. A few nights later I am not surprised when his mother calls. Before she moved to another town, Carol and I had met regularly to share our own stories and poems. Her voice sounds clear, but my mind trips over her words. "Mike's been missing since Thursday."

"I was just mentioning him in class this week," I tell her. "Remembering something he had written."

"I've filed a missing persons report," Carol says. My chest tightens. Mike is a gifted young man with a ready laugh, but he struggles with depression. I take a deep breath to push this weight away. "I'm trying to stay calm. I remember what you said."

Mike will be all right, I had told her. Because he writes.

All week I send out silent messages—to Mike, to my friends, people in my own family who are on difficult journeys. *You are loved. Be well. Be.* I seine the dark morning sky with nets of their remembered words. On Thursday afternoon Bonnie comes by to bring her portfolio in early; she has a work-related seminar and will miss finals week. "I want you to know—" She can't continue. "I showed the essay to my mom," she says, finally, "and she cried. It's brought me back to life, this paper. And I didn't intend to write about that. I thought I was just writing about moving, about boxing up my things for another moving day. I had no idea it was so important." She takes the Kleenex, embarrassed. "I'm thirty-five," she says, "and I didn't start to heal until I took that first writing class, remember? Three years ago. I had a diary when I was a little girl, but I quit writing, of course, after it happened. Writing—and I wanted to be a writer when I was a kid, but I hadn't thought about it for years, that was part of what was gone—" She stops, gathers herself. "Thank you," she says.

Early Saturday morning, the phone rings twice. The first voice is an editor of a small literary magazine in Montana. He has accepted a short story, one I called "Looking for the Killer." The second call is from Carol. The police have found Mike's body in his car, on a mountain overlooking the Pacific.

>–!–◆–○–◆–!–�

Christmas break, the building all but empty. I sit in my tiny office with an electric heater, the photos of Dean and our son Josh, and my mother's ancient shamrock plant, white blossoms still pushing against the window. My fingers rest on the computer keys. I need a new syllabus for next term's Writing 121. One that will work.

Searching Mike's room for something to hold onto, Carol has found a note: "Mother, will you please return these books to the library?" Ten words. Something presses on my sternum like the spread fingers of a hand.

An inversion has trapped thick winter fog over our valley; the roof of the art building next door and the sky beyond it look like silver extensions of my blank screen.

On the last morning of finals week, Eddie had turned in his paper. "The Story Tells Itself," this title penciled in calligraphy above a story he—or maybe some girl, someone who loves him—had carefully copied from the "Big Book" of Alcoholics Anonymous. That afternoon I had said goodbye to the woman who survived. "You have so many stories," I told her. "Do you see now? It's a collection." Bring the next one in, I had encouraged her. Share it with me. She nodded, once toward me, once toward her grandmother. But the term is over. I might never see her again.

"I need to be at the ocean for the Solstice," I tell Dean when I get home. The next morning we drive across the muted desert, the freeway barely visible as we dip into the tunnel of the Columbia Gorge, feeling its basalt walls through the fog and listening for the river. Then, amazed, we break into sunlight. The sky is a blue we have forgotten, the Douglas firs a green that makes us blink. As the winding Sunset Highway crests the Coast Range, we pass a small tree heavy with construction paper ornaments. Then another, and a third: surprises of color at the edge of the woods.

Only a half hour of this year's light remains by the time we reach the ocean. We spend it walking along the rim of land, as far west as we can go. There are no clouds between us and the sun dipping into the ocean just past Neahkanie Mountain.

Later, in the dark, we stumble through tufts of last summer's beach grasses and down the sandy trail to the water's edge. No moon; the stars seem to rise from the ocean itself. We tip our heads back, the surf a cushion of sound for balance. Dean lights a single candle. For a moment, brief in this current of cold ocean air, we have Solstice fire.

Economics

For years my idea of investing for the future was a passbook savings account. All I knew about the stock market was that my deposits weren't impressive enough to qualify for entry. T-bills, long-term bonds, balanced portfolios—none of these were ever discussed at my family's supper table. Although I did start a tax-sheltered savings plan when teachers were encouraged to do that, I didn't find time to research and open a Roth IRA until the only money I was actually earning were the few dollars I was getting paid for my writing. Still, I could transfer other savings to the Roth later, right? When my tax advisor learned of this venture into finance, he told me that I'd need to close out the Roth account as soon as possible, and pay a penalty. "No income," he explained. "Earned income—beyond your expenses." Oh.

Spending money, too, is a skill that has taken me years to learn. *What if we run out before the end of the month?* I was poor for a long time, and then in mid-career I was poor all over again. Things are better now; it's a bit easier to try on running shoes or wander through a bookstore. Dean buys me flowers. And thanks to that quitclaim deed, we have excellent credit. But we haven't yet cashed in on free airline miles, and neither of us knows our net worth.

I do know exactly how much my share of a group restaurant tab will be and how much money will remain in my pocket when we walk outside to our cars. I have never forgotten my wallet or realized as we tallied the bill that I was out of cash—though I envy the ones who can be this relaxed. I've heard stories about groups who decide to split the tab after most people have shared a couple of bottles of wine with their expensive meals while someone without enough money to pony up this kind of cash had been balancing angel hair pasta on her fork and sipping lemon water, but I have escaped this embarrassment. My friends are good people. Besides, if I don't have enough to cover that contingency, I probably won't be there.

It is hard to talk about money. Lacking it can feel awkward, having it when others don't can feel even more awkward. In a culture that measures our worth by our assets, I sometimes feel embarrassed that I don't really aspire to more money than I have. It would be great to travel more than I do, or to live in the country—country life has become a luxury I can't afford. So why haven't I figured out a way to make money? But what if the profits in my public employees retirement investments have come at someone else's expense? Does any good I might do with money really balance a tired assembly line worker's crushed fingers or the chicken packers who burned in that fire? Is it even possible to have a human-centered capitalism, a society with good schools, good food, and warm, safe homes for everyone? And sometimes I am completely blind-sided by economics. I can be walking beside a friend and suddenly feel a chasm split open between us, a glacial crevasse that is narrow enough to speak across—he may not even know that I'm teetering—but so deep that even a glance into its blue depths threatens to swallow me. Who knew that you could hire a coach to help your child select and gain admission to exactly the right college?

I was not at all surprised, though, when I heard a sociologist on National Public Radio concede that while studies repeatedly prove money does not correlate with happiness, the differences in wellbeing between those with yearly incomes of $5,000 and those with $50,000 are indeed distinct and measurable. Beyond $50,000, he said, it doesn't matter.

Maybe it was that man's voice, the kindness in it and the way he hesitated as if knowing that he might not be believed, that made me remember those three long days in Lewiston, the bigger town downriver from Orofino, when I was discovering some surprises of my own about money. John Steinbeck was still alive that July, though Faulkner had died the year before—something about a fall from a horse—and Hemingway the summer before that, when I was only sixteen. That headline had stretched across the top of the morning *Tribune* like a ribbon of black crepe, and there was a picture, too, that Papa Hemingway one with the big bear-like head emerging from a bulky turtleneck, his eyes looking directly at you. I felt as if I had stepped out onto a stair that wasn't there. A man can be destroyed but not defeated. "You know what this means," my Uncle Leonard said. "It's all over. For your generation, too."

I didn't know then that Hemingway's father had also shot himself, or how Emily, Leonard's mother and my mother's mother, had died, and of course I didn't know what was going to happen later. I was teetering along the edge of a drop-off, a sheer cliff of ignorance. But I still thought everything could be learned. I was going to find out what I needed to know. That's why I was waiting in a borrowed car outside the Lewiston County Club on that hot July day with the county library's copy of Faulkner's last book. I was babysitting, earning thirty dollars—the final thirty that would put me over the edge of the amount I needed to pay for the first year of college.

At the university, answers waited in the library stacks. Faulkner and Steinbeck and Hemingway himself, or at least the words they had left behind, and the words of Shakespeare and Homer too. Mr. Fleming's favorite, George Bernard Shaw. Poets—so many poets whose names I didn't yet know. But there would be teachers at the university who could tell me where to find them and how to decipher their secrets. Literature was the code, I was sure. It was a map, a guide to the secret of what it means to be human. How to live.

So why didn't everyone get to go to college, since it might be a matter of life and death? Economics was something else I didn't understand. But then, how could you hope to understand money if your family didn't have it?

It was hard to give my complete attention to *The Reivers;* I kept thinking about the kids, six of them—five girls and a boy, all between the ages of six and twelve, safely inside the gates of the country club now at their swimming lessons. From the outside, the country club was just a high brown wall. It was already getting hot in their mother's station wagon. She had shown me the way to the club and the corner market where I would stop on the way home for milk and bread (the kids could each have one Popsicle) and pointed out the huge plastic boxes by the washing machine—big as apple bins, one for colors, one for whites—and then she had waved goodbye from her friend's car as they backed rapidly out of the driveway. The great escape, she had called it. Three days in Seattle. Shopping, maybe—or just talking and eating lunch in some summery sidewalk café. Sleeping late. I opened the car door to catch any breeze that might be rising from the river. So far I hadn't made any mistakes.

When they came out of the country club they were hungry. Like a swarm of daddy long legs, all skinny arms and legs and empty stomachs, dragging damp towels almost as thin as the ones my family used. Four in the back seat, two in the front with me. The Popsicles were gone even before I had carried the milk out to the Family Market parking lot, and Allison was already opening the plastic bread wrapper. "Save some for sandwiches," I said. "Yeah," said Marcia. "Here." The faces in my rear view mirror sobered as she handed each child one slice. Gripping the wheel at the ten and two positions, I steered back up the hill to the huge house that looked out over the valley. A rich family's house, I thought. Their father, who would be home by six, was a banker.

The kids slid into their booth—I had never heard of a café booth in a house—and waited, slumped over the Formica tabletop, their thin arms stretched out ahead of them like a circle of tired basketball players too limp for a team cheer. I spread the peanut butter and Welches grape jelly. "That's what they'll want," their mother had said.

No nibbling around the crusts with this bunch. When the sandwiches were gone, the kids made themselves scarce. I put the milk glasses and plates in soapy water and stepped out into the back yard to check on things. Kevin was aiming a rubber-tipped arrow at a rainbow bull's-eye target propped against the lilac hedge. The six year old, the one they called Skeet, was reaching into the branches to retrieve an earlier miss. The other girls were playing some kind of tag game I couldn't quite follow. No, I decided—they were just chasing each other in short bursts of energy, then flopping down to lie on their backs in the shade or roll onto their stomachs in the mottled light at the edge of the lilac hedge, twisting their necks to check the backs of their arms. Sunbathing, I guessed. Kevin laid the bow down and joined them, leaving Skeet tangled in the lilac thicket. What's keeping them in this yard? I wondered. They must be so bored. What if they scatter, sprint off in six directions at once?

Cookies. If they were anything like my younger brothers at home... I had found a half bag of stale chocolate chips in the cupboard, and I knew my mother's recipe—my grandmother Emily's recipe—by heart. When I pulled the first cookie sheet from the oven, all six kids had caught the aroma and were schooled around me, reaching. "Wait! I made them for you, I'll just put them on this towel and you can all have some, don't burn—" But they had already pulled the hot cookies from the sheet and were stuffing them into their mouths, shaking their reddened fingertips. Skeet was jumping up and down, chocolate marking both corners of her mouth. "Missus Betty made cookies! Missus Betty made cookies!"

By the time we all sat down to the meatloaf their mother had told me to serve for dinner, the Quaker Oatmeal box recipe, I knew two things. They would eat every bite, despite the cookies. And their father would not be joining them. He was home, though. We could hear the sound of his coins on the tray; the back of his chair was nearly touching the head-high dividing wall behind the children's booth. He was examining tonight's bag of silver dollars, looking closely at their dates and treasury codes. He stopped by a teller's station on his way out the door each evening, he had told me by way of introducing himself, and traded one bag of coins for another. Should dinner wait, then, until he could join us? "Oh, God no," he said.

But as I rose to clear our plates he spoke again—*Kevin*—and the boy joined his father on the other side of the wall. None of the girls looked up. Nobody volunteered to help with dishes, but what kid would? They disappeared, downstairs maybe, or up in their rooms, parts of the house I had not seen. When I too stepped around the dividing wall to let the banker know I was leaving, I saw Kevin standing beside the big chair. His head was bent, trying to see through the magnifying glass in his father's hand. "See you tomorrow, then," I said. Neither of them answered.

Mourning doves were crying as I walked back up the hill to my aunt's house. Two more days. It seemed like a long time. But thirty dollars—that was good pay for babysitting. Last summer I had been paid only two dollars a day for taking care of a baby, and Dad had been angry about having to wait an extra half hour after his shift at the mill to give me a ride home. The eighty dollars I earned before I finally gave up that job felt tainted. It felt as if I had acquired them not by changing the little boy's diapers and feeding him his pabulum and trying to learn Spanish, checking my answers by turning a knob on a plastic box called a teaching machine, while he slept—both of us flushed with the summer heat in the little duplex—but by stealing part of each day's pay from the back pocket of someone else who was working a lot harder. Dad had to stand on his feet all day, lifting and turning and grading dimension lumber. No matter how hot it was, he wouldn't get out of the GMC pickup parked in front of the house. Finally the baby's mother would come home from work and I could walk out to the truck to join him.

Not that he'd talk. But at least, I thought, after our silent ride up the mountain there would be food on the supper table, maybe even the same meatloaf I had made for the doctor's family. Green beans from our garden, and new potatoes. Sliced tomatoes. Peach pie for dessert this time of year, or my favorite, chocolate cake. Maybe even ice cream. And no burned fingers.

Aunt Carolyn had iced tea waiting for me. Yes, I told her, I had found the country club and the market. The kids were okay. She had arranged this job for me. "I made cookies," I added.

"I'll bet they loved that," Carolyn said. Did she understand this family? I couldn't tell much from her voice. Skeet and her own little girl were friends, and she knew the children's mother too. But it was also true that she wanted me to be able to go to college almost as badly as I wanted to go. My mother had not gotten to go, and Carolyn hadn't either, though she had spent the first few years of her marriage sharing the joys of Married Student Housing with other young couples while her husband studied under the GI Bill. "So what did you think of Banker McDuck and his bag of silver dollars?" I laughed. Yes: Scrooge McDuck. Only two more days. I could do two more days.

Upstairs in the room I was sharing with little Molly, I sat on the floor in front of the full-length closet mirror with a pile of prickly metal curlers and a comb dipped into a glass of water. Molly lay on her stomach on the carpet beside me. "I've got to figure out how to get these curlers in my hair," I told her. "I don't know why it's so hard—everything seems backwards." I stuck the pink plastic pin into the first curler, but when I released my hold on it the curler tilted out just above my left ear like a rocket. "Cape Canaveral! Three two one LIFTOFF!" Molly giggled. Wouldn't it be fun, I thought, to have a little sister? Molly and I were separated by the same amount of years as our mothers—Carolyn had been the little sis, lying awake to hear Mom's whispered secrets. Molly sat with me now, chattering through the hour it took to do what was a ten-minute job for my mother. Lord knows what I'll look like in the morning, I thought as we pushed the stuffed animals onto the floor and lay back on the pillows. Headlights from the cars still traveling up the steep street played across the ceiling. I had to figure out how to do my own hair—I couldn't take Mom with me to college. "I wish you could stay all summer," Molly said sleepily. "I wish you lived with us."

What I was really going to miss, I thought as I waited for sleep, was not Mom putting the curlers in my hair and the scalp-prickly feeling I loved, but the way her voice seemed part of her hands. The way we seemed almost to meld into one person. If I were home tonight I would be telling her about the coins, and the country club. The cookies.

It was while Mom was setting my hair, a quiet mid-morning last summer with all three boys playing outside, that I learned what had happened to my grandmother. I knew that Emily had died before I was born, when Carolyn was barely a teenager. I didn't know yet that Mom, whose own first baby had not yet learned to sit up, had also been too young to lose a mother. Of course I understood that my grandmother's death had left my mother sad. And I wished I could have met her. But I did not know, at seventeen, that my own mother's quiet voice would be the life raft that kept me afloat through my thirties, my forties, even after my own hair glowed white in all the family photos.

"Mom, what did your mother die of? Heart failure?" I had asked her. The comb slipped against my scalp. "Yes," she said after a moment. "That's what it was." I waited, feeling that mixture of curiosity and guilt that was such a part of who I was: the one who needed to know things. When the curlers were all in place, she said, "Come outside." We sat down at the picnic table under the fir tree. What could be too big to say aloud in the kitchen where the morning's bread dough was already rising in the yellow bowl? My brothers were pulling the battered wagon up the rocky driveway behind the bicycle, their voices muffled by the noise. "She didn't really die of heart failure." Mom sounded as if she had been holding her breath, swimming underwater for a long time. "I shouldn't have said that." Then her words came all at once, as if there were no spaces between them. "Mama took her own life." I reached across the table for her hand. "Oh, Mom," I said.

"I'm sorry," she told me. "I'm so sorry." She was crying now. "I didn't want you to be hurt. I wanted to protect you from it, but that was wrong."

⊱—⊹⟡⊹—⊰

People didn't talk much about depression in 1962. But I had already sensed that, in spite of the stories I'd been told about my grandmother's sense of humor, she had had plenty of reasons to be sad. Once she had begged her husband for two quarters: as a man, of course, all the money was his. Emily, who had grown up on the Atlantic, was so homesick for the sea—and for 50 cents, the train would carry her from their small town in Oregon to the Pacific and back again. She would be home in time to have his dinner waiting. No, he told her. No.

What if he had said yes? I wondered. What would have been spent, what saved?

In my last year of high school one of the teachers showed us a film about mental illness. A woman stood up in a movie theater, screaming, and ran straight into the arms of an usher. In the next scene she woke in a hospital, white-suited doctors looking down at her. That winter, when I lay staring into darkness, my mother came to sit on the edge of the bed. "Listen to this," she said, and read me poems by Robert Frost, "Two Look at Two," or "Birches," until I could feel the panic melting. I could feel her hand on my back, steady and warm. "You'll be all right," she said.

And she convinced me to spend some of my savings—five dollars a month—to order a portable typewriter from the Sears catalog. I wasn't easily persuaded, though I yearned for that typewriter. Every writer had one. But I had practiced resolve until I could almost feel it, like a hammered-thin steel wire running up my spine and out through my neck and arms and legs. I had said no to Milk Duds when the eighth grade class was treated to a movie matinee. No to cheeseburgers and cherry Cokes on band trips. No warm winter coat. I wore jersey work gloves to school. No records, no radio. I missed the senior formal dance, and I felt a half-step off the path as I walked between our health and government classes beside the kids I had gone to school with all my life. I didn't even know what Rainbow Girls did, or why only some girls were asked to join—"Shhhh—it's a secret," Pam told me once when I wondered aloud. I had no idea what was in *Seventeen* magazine.

Would there have been another way to get to college? When you are focusing as hard as I was, it does not occur to you that other possibilities exist and perhaps in some strange way you are drawing even more limits around your life. Should I have risked the application fees to schools like Stanford and Whitman and the University of the Pacific on the chance that if I got accepted, I'd get enough scholarship money and actually get to go? But if I paid these application fees, $25 to each school, I wouldn't have enough left in my savings for the first year at the University of Idaho, where I would have to pay for books and room and board, but not tuition. I didn't know, and there was no one to ask. Our school counselor had scoffed when I told him my parents would not be able to help me with the costs of college. Maybe he thought I was lying. "If I can't help my little girl when she's 18, I'll be a total failure as a father," he said.

On the bus ride home from my three-day job, I cradled a heavy bundle—thirty silver dollars—in my lap. My aunt had tied them into a white handkerchief, but they kept trying to spill out past the knot. "If you're smart you'll save these," the banker had told me. "They'll be worth more in a few years." These were among the last of the dollars minted without the copper sandwich core. But of course I would have to add them to my savings account to pay the fall semester's dormitory fee. "It takes money to make money." I could almost hear my father's bitter voice, see his shoulders hunching over figures scrawled on the back of an envelope or one of his children's school papers.

Outside the window of the old bus—a rusty white, with Clearwater Stage Line painted in green letters along the side—the river carried last winter's snowmelt back toward Lewiston and on toward the Pacific. What did the future hold for those hungry kids? The night before, as we had been finishing our last supper together, I had urged them to take just one or two of that day's cookies—peanut butter this time—and pass the plate around the table. They could each have all they wanted, I said. I would refill the plate. I had made a double batch, and there were more cookies in the jar.

"You might as well give up," their father had said from behind his barrier wall. "It's a hopeless cause." We were wedged so tightly in the booth that we had flinched as one.

I squinted against the sunlight reflecting from the water's surface, fighting back nausea from the diesel fumes. In the places where the water eddied, the water was dark green. But in early January when my grandmother had jumped into this river, the water would have looked black from the bridge. If a person imagines blankness, nothing, a river-deep escape from hopelessness, I wondered, do her children disappear from her consciousness as well? Or is she simply unable to care? Maybe the pain she will leave behind doesn't seem real to her.

I would be asking these questions again, shouting them against the roof of sleep when my father died, and Uncle Leonard too. But I didn't know that yet. I didn't even know, that day, that ignorance can be a blessing.

A few weeks later Martin Luther King spoke from the steps of the Lincoln Memorial, and after that I left for college. I found a job in the dormitory kitchen, and summer waitress work. The spring that I earned my degree, one Oregon school district was recruiting teachers by offering them membership in a country club, but I walked past their table and filled out an application for the small school on the Yakama Indian Reservation. I lived on toast and coffee in the back of the general store, saving money again, this time for graduate school. There was so much I still needed to learn.

Then came the decades in all those other classrooms, passing on the stories. Hemingway and Steinbeck and even Faulkner's words were dimmer now, their names overshadowed by Toni Morrison and Tillie Olsen, James Baldwin, Lucille Clifton and Simon Ortiz, Leslie Marmon Silko, so many others; and of course the stories had turned out to hold more questions than answers. But sometimes when I watched one of my community college students sitting stunned and silent—some woman whose voice would break when she tried to speak: "I didn't know anyone else ever felt like this!"—I knew she was clinging to the same thread of words that I had clung to, gasping above the rocky currents of her life. One boy carried his literature book in an old cigar box to keep the corners from fraying in his daypack, and he didn't want anyone else to touch it.

For a while I tried to save any silver dollars that came my way in a Mason jar, but before the end of the month I would be handing them across a grocery counter. Or giving them to the taxi driver when, in one of those week-before-payday droughts familiar to all teachers, my car wouldn't start and I had to get to school on time. Not long ago, though, one of my brothers reached into a drawer and brought out a Lady Liberty dollar that was exactly one hundred years old. "Here," he said. "Now you'll never be broke."

I wondered sometimes whether Skeet and Kevin and the other children got to go to college. Having money, I knew now, was no guarantee. Years later, though I could not have imagined such a thing on the bus ride home that afternoon, I would find myself passing along my mother's first wheelchair to these children's mother, who was still Aunt Carolyn's friend.

The banker had long since disappeared from her life and she was poor now too. Those silver-spoked wheels, she told Carolyn, would open whole new possibilities. It was as close as I would come to understanding economics.

Body Mechanics

Swimming

The swimming pool was in the basement of the men's gym. It was a huge gray building with gargoyles for rainspouts, and the best athlete in the school lived as high above the swimming pool as you could get, up in one of the gothic towers, because his family was poor and he couldn't afford housing. At least that was the story. Sort of a room in the attic, in a building that looked more like a cathedral than a gym. People said he actually did his own schoolwork, even in classes where he got D's. Once I was stepping up onto the curb in the hurried ten-minute crush between classes just as he was stepping down, and my eyes were exactly level with his belt buckle. I couldn't help looking on up, craning my neck the way you do when the sign says "Largest White Pine in the World," even as I wondered how it would feel to have people staring at your body with their mouths open. Everywhere you went, every minute. Except in that little tower. Maybe God looks like this, I thought, complete with the human camouflage of a left leg slightly shriveled from childhood polio. Even with that mortal touch, this guy could do things on the track and football field that we had never seen any other human do. Sometimes, on my way up the steps of the men's gym, I used to imagine him in his little tower room, probably a little stone cell with a cot his feet would stick out of. A thin slit of a window too high for anyone to see in. At peace, but absolutely alone. He would play for the Redskins for nearly a complete season before someone crushed his knee beyond repair, and when the papers carried the story of how he had died of sickle cell anemia before he was forty they also said he had spent his life working with children in Washington DC, where his family lived. Although, the story said, he had been sick for a long, long time.

Women were only allowed in the men's gym during certain hours and we were restricted to the dressing room and the long dark stairs down to the pool. You don't want to be caught in here at the wrong time, the Physical Education director told us. Men are required to take swimming too, and they swim nude. We felt pretty nude ourselves. They made us check out a faded blue or red cotton suit before every class, but everything felt pretty visible, even before the suits got wet. "The Kleenex suits," people called them. Why was it okay, even required, for men to take their swim class without trunks and unthinkable for us? "Wouldn't that be weird, coming to class naked?" someone said. There was giggling. Still, some of the guys must have had to get used to it too. I wondered what it would feel like, swimming with no suit on.

I was as embarrassed as everybody else in the Kleenex suits, or more so. I suppose the girls with small breasts were as self-conscious as the ones with large breasts, but the suits definitely covered more of what they were embarrassed about. Did they make us wear those suits to help us learn to accept our bodies, a sort of sink or swim teaching technique? Or maybe it was more like a drill sergeant's reminder of how far we had yet to come, what chunks of raw human flesh they had to work with. It helped a little when I took my glasses off and put them in my locker. Everybody looked the same to me then, some blobs larger than others is all.

It's hard to hear when you can't see, I discovered, especially when you're blinking water out of your eyes in an echoing basement pool and your teacher has a Virginia way of pronouncing words. "Swim down to the white line," Miss Tuttle said once, and I churned away, yards after everyone else had stopped at the white lion's head decorating the edge of the pool. Even with the gargoyles, I had no inkling I was in the presence of African animals down here. Things got a bit easier after she said I could wear my glasses in the pool, but not much.

I loved it. Even with the flimsy suits and the walk back to the dorm in the snow with my hair still damp, all those things people complained about so steadily. I was pretty sure I understood the university's Phys Ed requirements. A semester of swimming, a semester of dance, a team sport, an individual sport. When we emerged at the end of our sophomore year, ready to take the real classes in our majors, we would be able to move through the world in any direction. You couldn't throw anything at us that we couldn't catch or at least sidestep. We would know how to live in our bodies. In 1963 nobody had said anything about our bodies being ourselves. It was because of our bodies that we had to be protected from ourselves. *In loco parentis* meant the dorm doors locked at 10:00 and didn't open again until 6:30. Our bodies were the reason that only women had to sign up for Healthful Living during the first semester. I was one of the lucky ones who scored over 80 on the initial test so I got to drop it and take philosophy instead, and missed a lot of talk about personal hygiene and watching old Miss Betts crouching on top of her desk on her hands and knees to demonstrate the sure cure for cramps, but I got the message that only women needed to learn how to live healthily. None of us could escape all the talk about those three numbers that added up to whatever your fate was going to be. (36, 27, 39.) And everybody knew this much: at any moment your body could detonate something like a lab explosion that could scar you forever. "It's just chemical," Mom had already explained. "Men react like that."

But the P.E. requirements seemed like a promise of better things to come. I suppose I thought if I could learn to do the things in these Phys Ed classes my body would finally be at home in the world. There were so many places I wanted to go, and I wasn't at all sure how to get to them. I started with swimming because I wanted to walk beyond my father's voice ("Don't go in above your knees. That current will pull you under!") right out into the river the way I'd watched my mother do once. Swim clear across.

⊱⊰⊹⊱⊰⊹⊱⊰

My friend Katharine has a swimming pool in her house at the beach. I forgot to pack a suit, but she has left the pool uncovered especially for me so I put on my thinnest shorts and tank top and step in. The water is just right, and I can see the Lodgepoles outside the windows. It's a two-lane lap pool. Katharine is inside the open glass doors, listening to the evening news, her chair pushed close to the television so she can catch the outlines of the images. I know she can't see this far, but I roll on my back and float, trying to show her that I'm happy to be here, finally sharing this pool she has loved so much. On the wall of her English Department office there's a picture of her small daughter underwater, going down and down, her hands at her sides and her eyes open, a smiling little minnow. "Now That's Water!" says the caption.

The daughter is bigger now, twelve. I have taken her to her dance class many times in the last few months, when Katharine has been unable to drive. It's small town stuff; nobody from the dry side of our state will be going on to Juilliard. Katharine says she just wants the girl to feel at home in her body.

I turn, reach out into a crawl. I still don't exhale completely and run into breathing trouble when I swim. I can hear voices from the television, blurred a little as I dip my head back under. "Now that's water!" is what the woman who taught Katharine's daughter to swim had said three weeks before she died of the brain tumor that grew out of nowhere and blocked her ability to remember the language of the world. Her friends had brought her to the pool and helped her in, and language, and joy, came back one last time. Three words. A wonderful woman, Katharine had told me, tears spilling. The friends had used her daughter's picture and the water words printed on T-shirts to help raise money for hospital bills.

And now something has been pressing on Katharine's optic nerve, and the doctors have reached as delicately as they could into that deep space behind the eyes, those tangled mysteries. She is still in great pain. "Nights are the worst," she tells me. "Maybe in the morning I'll feel better, and we can talk."

I turn over, trying to let the water bear me up.

>⋅⬧⋅○⋅⬧⋅◁

By the end of the Beginning Swimming class we could tread water for five minutes in the deep end and Miss Tuttle had showed us how to keep from drowning by grasping our knees and rolling into a ball, face down. It seemed backwards to me and sometimes, holding my breath and looking down into that darkness, I knew why so many people in the class were still battling a fear of the water. But we had all learned to dive from the edge of the pool—hips up, chin down—and on the last day of class we were to dive in and swim to the far end. Before we started she picked out a group of us to dive several times. It's like Plato in my philosophy class, I thought. Beauty is truth, truth beauty. You just think of the ideal and your body makes a form of it. Probably she was letting us feel this one more time, letting the others feel it by watching us. Finally she had us dive in and swim to the end. "Again," she said when I pulled myself out, gasping. I walked back, dripping. Someone was holding my glasses, which had fallen off and had to be rescued from the black bottom of the deep end the day we learned to dive from the board and I had forgotten I had them on. I dove again. Chin down, hips up, hands together. Pull. "D," she said, when I finally reached the ladder. She made a mark on her clipboard.

Maybe it was because of her honesty that we all loved her. "Don't believe everything you read in the *Reader's Digest*," she told us—exactly the kind of thing that people said at home. I copied her advice onto an index card and hung it from the piece of driftwood with the words of wisdom I was picking up in my Humanities class. Miss Tuttle was amazed when she substituted for the intermediate swim class teacher the next semester and found me clinging to the edge of the pool as she took roll. "What are you doing here?" she said.

Our new teacher, Jenny, was fun too. She would get into the pool and demonstrate each stroke, then watch us and cheer. "That was wonderful!" she'd say. Intermediate Swimming was a lot more relaxed than beginner's class. We could swim, right? We'd all line up on the edge of the concrete, our legs in the water, to watch her demonstrate one more time. We were doing everything right except we should move our arms this way, our legs more like this, hold our heads and hands and feet like this. We laughed. "So what were we doing right?" "No, no, you were really wonderful," she would say. Every time. Jenny was a lesbian. Of course we didn't call her by her first name but I can't remember her last name, Dr. somebody. My new roommate, who was also a lesbian, told me about Jenny. She owned a home with another woman and besides, Beth said, you can always tell by the eyes. It was a secret I had to keep, Jenny's and Beth's too. I had no idea what lesbians did with their bodies. Jenny's looked beautiful in the water, patient and symmetrical in all the strokes. Beauty is truth.

"Don't worry," Beth had told me on the day I suddenly knew she was a lesbian. "I'm not attracted to you." She was putting curlers in her hair, and she had to twist around to talk to me over her shoulder.

You could go over to the men's gym and practice on Saturday mornings and I had to do that to pass Intermediate Swimming. Beth gave me books to look at, little diagrams of the strokes with arrows to show the direction of the kicks, but they didn't seem to help much. I didn't breathe right and I wheezed so loudly it scared people. And there were strange strokes where you used the scissors kick from the sidestroke but the arm stroke from the Australian crawl. It was like trying to pat your head and rub your stomach in ten feet of water. What if I flunked P.E.? Miss Tuttle had been right. One morning I thrashed up to a slim and brilliant girl from my hometown. Her father owned a mill; she had been a lifeguard at our pool and a Homecoming princess too. "Bette, you're trying too hard," she said.

⊱ ❧ ⊰

We took our son into the apartment pool when he was four months old, riding on his father's shoulders, laughing. The next summer in mother-child swimming lessons I learned to let him go underwater. He was so happy below the surface, a slippery little fish. We would toss him back and forth, laughing. Even during the winter he would run straight down the bank of any river and out into the water, over his head, shivering happily when we dragged him out. By the time he was seven, though still the size of a five year old, he had passed the test to swim in the deep end of the hot springs pool. Only then did he come up for air on his own without my hand pushing, reminding him that he was one of us, the lunged ones. But he loved to jump off the high platform and stay down by the big boulders on the bottom while I counted and counted, if I got to 50 I'd yell for the lifeguard—44, 45—and he'd pop up, laughing.

I was right about two things, he would tell me much later. The swimming lessons, and that tattoo.

Team Sport

They called it your team sport requirement but whether you took basketball or softball or field hockey, you had to spend the first nine weeks in Body Mechanics. There was even a text for this course, a hand-lettered pamphlet with line drawings of women's shapes—endomorphs, mesomorphs, ectomorphs—and diagrams of the exercises. The woman who taught basketball and Body Mechanics was tall and slim and pretty. An ectomorph. We lay on the gym floor and pumped our legs as if we were riding an upside down bicycle and then watched while she demonstrated how to feel the chair with your calf, then sit without looking behind you. These are things a lady knows, she said.

Lady was one of the passwords of the P.E. department. All right, ladies. Time to go. Eugenie turned around once and yelled back across the gym, "Dammit, I ain't no lady!"

We weren't Majors, either. In the Women's Gym, Major meant P.E. major. They had pale blue shorts instead of dark navy like the rest of us. The Minors wore them too. I was just as glad not to have the pale blue shorts even though the people who wore them were all mesomorphs and knew how to swing their legs and take the wooden bars three at a time, and nobody ever said to them, "You know, balance can be improved." People in the pale blue shorts were scrutinized carefully. "They have a file on all the Majors," Beth said. "Everything about you is in that file." She had been sent home for two years because of what was in hers. She was very careful.

But once the silent treatment got to her and she asked Eugenie to be her partner in the badminton doubles tournament. Eugenie has no depth perception. Sure, she said. At least the shuttlecock doesn't break your glasses when it hits you in the face. The tournament went on for three weeks. Eugenie was actually pretty good with the serves that came to her right side and let her locate them in space before she swung. "Got it!" Beth would yell, swooping in whenever the shuttlecock came straight at Eugenie, who stood in one spot in her wrinkled PE shirt and shorts and her endomorphic happiness, flaunting the rules about weekly ironing of the uniform and squeaking something like, "Oh! Oh!" And then, "Good one,

Beth!" People in pale blue shorts glared. There was no stopping this team. And Eugenie's name would be on the trophy.

Once I came into my dorm room and saw the girl who lived on the other side of the sleeping porch standing naked in front of the mirror. "What are you doing?" I asked her. "Just looking at myself," she said. She was still smiling.

"What's *wrong* with her?" I asked Eugenie.

Basketball was a disappointment. It was hard to feel the magic of those seventh grade lunch hours when the boys had welcomed me to their sweaty, red-faced game even though I had to wear a dress in junior high: these women's rules wouldn't let you dribble more than twice or cross the center line. Two forwards waited at one end and two guards stayed at the other. One player could "rove," but you had to keep rotating. Women don't have the stamina to play full court, our teacher told us. I remembered the answer to our high school plea for a real basketball team: "Idaho frowns on competitive sports for women." Why, why? How could a state frown, anyway? But that's all Mrs. Hargrave would say. She had taught at this university, too, before she married and came to our town to teach high school P.E.; I recognized her maiden name on the cover of the Body Mechanics book.

There was a playday, though, a Women's Recreation Association gathering at Columbia Basin College across the Washington desert from us, and not one of the Majors had the GPA to be eligible. So there we were, a couple of Minors and a handful of baggy navy blue short wearers, circling the two girls who crouched down to wait for the jump ball. When it came to me I used the one skill our slim, pretty teacher had taught us. Two steps, one hand under the ball, one hand on top, right knee goes up. I don't think anyone even tried to stop me. We won, 12-8.

Three years later I was the assistant basketball coach for the first girls' team in the high school where I was teaching literature and something I was supposed to call Composition. The head coach was the girls' P.E. teacher, the only other young woman on the staff. We spent our mornings in the gym where the boys were shooting around before the first bell, learning about something called backspin. "Put a little English on it, Thoreau," the boys teased me. Even the P.E. teacher had no idea what they were talking about.

Dance

Twiggy was the ideal. We stared at her picture, incredulous, but we wouldn't hear the word anorexia for another decade. Bulimia came even later, though I do remember a girl telling me all you had to do was put your finger in your throat and throw up and you could eat as much as you wanted. It was easy, she said. A perfect solution. I tried it once, but I couldn't quite do it. Maybe because of that time I'd choked on the orange slice and Dad had to jam his finger into my throat.

Everybody gained ten pounds in the first year of college, even though there was never enough to eat. The older girls had already prepared us; it was because the food was so starchy, they said. By the time these upperclassmen arrived that first September we had already been sleeping in the dorm for nearly a week, but no meals were served during freshman orientation. We had shared our apples and cookies from home until they ran out, and then we just waited. Buckwheat pancakes, the menu posted on the bulletin board said. Two days to go. My mouth still does funny things when I hear those words, even though these buckwheat pancakes turned out to be thin hard wafers nothing like what my family called hotcakes.

Once, when the dining room server set a plate down in front of a girl, she vomited into it. "It's about time!" someone said just loudly enough for everyone to hear. The food was truly terrible, probably the same kind you get in women's prisons where the food is cheap: the pizza had leftover scrambled eggs in it, for instance. The girl had run through the rows of tables and out the door. "She was sick, that's all," I said. I wondered how she would be able to come back the next night. You never knew what your body was going to do, what embarrassing trouble it could get you into at any moment. The housemother looked furious.

It took me a long time, years, to realize that there was nothing wrong with the girl who stood in front of the mirror looking at her body.

I would have skipped the dance semester of Phys Ed if I could. No way could I imagine myself moving across the creaky old women's gym floor in a black leotard. Once Dad had seen me reflected in the window when I was trying to get a towel out of the drawer after a bath. I was fourteen. "Well, you look pretty much the same as when you were little," he said. "Same parts, just more of them." My mother had put her arms around me and glared at him. But I was already moving around like a crippled cow that summer, slumping into clothes so loose I could pretend I was invisible.

In folk dance you just wore your P.E. uniform. It was kind of strange, 30 girls in blue shorts dancing with each other. But once we got over the awkwardness it was fun. I loved the Jewish song for water, reaching into the circle with our arms raised, then backing out. And a Russian dance with lots of stomping in a ring. It's all about community, Miss Tuttle said. I was happy to find her teaching something besides swimming. Folk dance reminded me of square dancing after the 4-H meetings when I was junior high age and wanting to be close to boys but a little scared too. Feeling their callusy hands on the do-si-dos and their arms touching mine on the allemande lefts, and that centrifugal pull toward something that made my heart pound on the swing-your-partners. And, thank God, it wasn't anything like the high school dances that next year where I had sat on the folding chair behind the crepe paper in the dark or, finally, moved my feet stiffly along beside the boy whose hand was on my back. I knew what had happened between junior high and high school but I didn't know what to do about it. The man who'd been like a second father to me, our 4-H leader and Sunday School teacher, had twisted around in the saddle and kissed me on the mouth. He had known me since I was a baby.

Things could turn on you, that's all I knew for sure.

"Hump day, folks," Miss Tuttle said one morning when she walked in. We were sprawled out on the mats at the edge of the gym, waiting for her. Wednesday. Halfway through the week. We grinned back at her. That was the day she made me demonstrate Tinikling, to prove to the others that it could be done. It was a Polynesian dance; you had to step between two clashing sticks in a pattern I had carefully memorized. Maybe she remembered her swimming comment and was trying to make up for it. But it didn't feel like dancing, the way I was sure it felt to the people whose dance it was. It felt mechanical. Just a matter of counting, and maybe being more alert than the others, more aware of things that can come at you from the side.

That spring Miss Tuttle left the University to go live with her family in Virginia. She wasn't old enough to retire from teaching, but she had a terminal kind of diabetes, Beth said. First she would lose her sight.

>—⊶⊷•O•⊶⊷—◁

Sometimes Dean and I do what he calls bear dancing. We just hold each other and lean one way and then the other, stomping as hard as we want to.

It's love, of course, that makes any kind of dancing possible. I remember the miracle of it, that someone loved my body and thought it was perfect.

"She has the body of a truck, but her breasts are surprisingly firm," a former boyfriend had once told someone. Jesus, the things we do to each other.

I remember walking in the early morning light from the bed to the bathroom, naked, wondering: can it possibly be true? Even if I don't look like the pictures in the magazines? By the time I had met the man who would become my husband I was nearly 27, and I had finally had a couple of fumbling attempts at relationships. But this was a new world. My body felt new, too. As if I had thrown off the morning covers and discovered brand new legs and arms and breasts, a new stomach rising with each breath. Maybe this is the secret, I remember thinking. A spark comes out of nowhere and ignites this mystery that the body makes visible. Eyelashes, fine strands of hair, smooth and mysteriously folding places on our skins. And invisible, too. Love sent us so deep into our bodies that we left them behind, let us go to a place where there was no skin, no bone, nothing to hold upright.

Childbirth led to miracles of its own. *So here's what the body does.* It fades after the months of expanding and the exquisite labor and the nursing, this awareness, but it never completely leaves you either. Why had I ever been embarrassed about my body? I wondered. This swelling center where I could feel him swimming. These breasts that he reached for, mouth open, these hips he fit over so perfectly. That amazing, yawning core from which he had emerged, that precious head. It seemed as silly as a river's being afraid of its own current.

Individual Sport

"She's the kind of woman you would have to go to a bowling alley to encounter." It's a line from a Dudley Moore comedy; the kind of line that sticks in your mind and becomes a family joke even if nobody can quite remember the reference. And it's funny, but I would have to live almost half of my life to know why. When they built the bowling alley the year I was eleven, I had thought maybe bowling was something our family could aspire to. The town kids talk about their parents' bowling leagues had made it sound downright glamorous. And it was new. Everybody would be starting at the same place. We could be like other people, I thought. Dad just shook his head and made that sound. Psshh.

Because of that extra semester of swimming, I was a junior when I got to my individual sport and had to choose between "badminton and fencing" or "tennis and bowling." I agonized. How could I turn down a chance to wrap my head and body like a white chrysalis and lunge at the world with a silver foil, one arm arced above my head? In the end, though, it was bowling. And tennis, in nearly-white shoes.

My highest bowling score was 125, and when I got back to the dorm Beth said no, that can't be right. Sure enough, I had made a mistake on the scorecard. But someone had showed me how to hold the ball and I'd felt it, that body knowledge when the ball leaves your hand and you know it's a strike long before it hits. You can turn your back and walk away, and you know. Then the sound.

None of us did as well at tennis. There were too many of us in the class and we spent too much time chasing balls that went over the fence. It seems funny to me now that the Phys Ed department combined bowling and tennis, the sports of Archie Bunker and the country club. Maybe that's what they wanted us to learn.

>–I–◆›–O–‹◆–I–◄

After that college P.E. class I have only been bowling three times. Twice we took our son when he was four. He ran and pushed the ball mightily out into the gutter, and came back smiling. "Just right," he said. Then we got ice cream cones at the counter. It was a two-lane alley in the small town where I was teaching then, dark and incredibly dirty, but he had been begging us to take him. A few people sat at tables in the next room drinking coffee with their doughnuts and ignoring the flies. "Mom, you should be the ice cream lady at the bowling alley," my son said. That would be a lot more fun than having a mom who was a teacher, he figured.

The last time I went bowling I rode in a hospital van with the alcoholics from the fourth floor rehab. I was the only patient on the third floor, what they called the stress center, and they sent me along on this social therapy trip designed to show alcoholics that they can have fun without drinking. I had gone into the stress center during Christmas break as a desperate ploy to force social services to help our son, whose teenage years had carried him so deeply into alcohol and drugs that we were sure he was going to die. The social workers had already told us, twice, that he undoubtedly would die and they hoped he would do it soon and we'd get out of their hair. If I wasn't home, they'd have to help him, I thought. Already, though, I knew this was a mistake. I just wanted to find my son and hold his thinning body in my arms, Merry Christmas, Merry Christmas, even if he would be out the window and lost to the street the minute I let go, for three weeks, six weeks, maybe forever. But here I was in the blue van, going bowling with Erik—

the spiked-haired sixteen year old who called the young activities director "Crystal Meth"—and a quietly embarrassed older woman who pointed out her house to me as we drove past it, a couple of starting-to-gray guys in Levis and sweatshirts, and Crystal herself. We trooped into the bowling alley—a strange place to take alcoholics in the early stages of recovery, I remember thinking. Aren't bowling alleys associated with beer? The rental shoes smelled funny and didn't quite fit. Christmas Eve, four o'clock. We had the bowling alley to ourselves.

Not one of us could bowl worth a damn. Erik's style was the craziest, of course—it looked more like fast-pitch softball than bowling, accompanied with wild whoops and body gestures to push the ball over, over. Pretty soon everybody was laughing and Crystal had lost track of the score. "He's not ready yet," the older woman whispered to me. But she didn't stop looking at Erik, or smiling.

⊱━◆━◉━◆━⊰

When I graduated from college with a 4.0—not that uncommon today but unusual in 1967—I was supposed to send a profile photograph to the artist who would sculpt a bronze head for the plaque in the library. But I had seen the other eleven heads on that plaque up close. They looked lumpy and slightly green, lonesome for the bodies they belonged to. I didn't send a picture. What did a 4.0 mean, after all? That you were desperate for learning; you needed to know everything. (What's so funny about the name Forney Hall? some of us had asked during our first hungry week. Horny Forney, that's what's so funny. That's what people call us. —What does "horny" mean?)

And, of course, getting a 4.0 also meant you'd had some lucky breaks. One of them was simple: they gave written tests in the P.E. classes, so if you could remember what they meant by "love" you might get an A even if you couldn't play tennis.

When I came back from student teaching to join my friends on campus for the final winter term, my friend Lydia was the one who broke the news: I had been tapped for I-Club, the Women's Recreation Honorary. Only Majors got in, and occasionally Minors. They wore special gray blazers with an "I" stitched on the pocket and assisted the P.E. department when high school girls came on campus for a playday. Beth had accepted the "I" for me, Lydia said, at the awards ceremony. "Serious as all hell, of course," Lydia laughed. We spoke the same language, Lydia and I, though her large, poor family was black and from New York while mine was white and here in Idaho. I remembered how Beth had walked home from the gym with Eugenie, planning the strategy for the next badminton match. "Not a trace of a smile," Eugenie would confide later. "It's as if she really thinks I'm an equal partner." Me? I-Club? I asked Lydia. It had to be a joke. By now both of us were rolling on the bunk, helpless with laughter. "No," gasped Lydia, when she finally caught her breath. "Turns out there are four qualifications—points for participating, sportsmanship, academics, and ability. But they can waive one of them, and in your case they waived ability." We howled. I must have had more points for attendance at the Women's Recreation hour than any other person on campus. It's true, I was always there.

>⦁⦁⦁O⦁⦁⦁<

At the community college, everybody wants to take P.E. The Phys Ed department calls it Lifelong Learning. They offer everything from scuba diving to yoga for one credit, though weight training and walking are the most popular. The girls who look like that lifeguard from my hometown all want to take Abs-to-Die-For, and men take it too. "I'll need a P.E. class," students say when advisors are filling out schedules. It's not required; they just mean that between their jobs and kids and commutes, a P.E. class is their ticket to survival. Kickboxing fills up fast, and Aquatics for Arthritics usually has a waiting list.

Until the doctor told me, well, if your ankle hurts, don't do it, I was one of those people who couldn't wait to start the day with a five mile run. Technically, it was jogging—I wasn't fast—but I still have dreams about running, skimming along under the morning stars. Like flying, only lower. Once in a while our son, who is whole and safe and healthy at last, joins me for a hike in the High Wallowas just as we used to do every summer, the two of us, when he was growing up. Even though I'm usually huffing and puffing up the trail and carrying the weight of human survival on my back, that feels like flying too.

And sometimes, alone at a mountain lake or river, I step into the water and feel its current touching my whole body at once.

We took my father backpacking when he was 65, and I have a picture of him with his hat cocked over one eye, grinning at the camera. The same man who could put his hand on a fencepost and vault over, just a bit of gray in his hair, that's all. But it was only months before the emphysema and the trailing green oxygen tubes and the Prednisone that would twist his back with another kind of weight. Once he stood at the bottom of his porch steps, his hand on my arm as he waited to catch his breath. "We sure got old fast, didn't we?" he said. That same grin, but embarrassed, surprised.

When I hold my mother in my arms, careful not to squeeze too hard, I think: this is coming. Machines can tell you things about your bones now that you may not want to know. Sometimes I panic. Does that twinge in my hip mean I'll need hip replacement surgery, the kind I watched her go through twice? Sometimes I am just confused. Who is that white-haired woman in the window reflection? And she's wearing my hat!

But my concept of beauty keeps changing, too. After my son was born, in a family pattern opposite of the norm, I lost those 15 pounds I had been so worried about. People still startle me when they say I'm small, and I was simply amazed when the Pilates instructor announced that if she had a body like mine, she would never wear what I was wearing—sweatpants and a shirt. She'd come to class in a body leotard, she said. But long ago I quit thinking much about scales. I look at other things. My mother's skin—so soft, like water. Her eyes, her smile. "You're beautiful!" my sister and I said in one voice when we saw her 65th class reunion picture. She looked at us, astonished.

In the mornings now, I practice T'ai Chi, trying to learn to move with my whole body. I'm one of the youngest people in the class. Thirty or so people started, but most of them dropped out early, while Tom was still telling us that it would take a while to learn to tell rapture from pain. Dale and Barbara are in their 70's, Jim is retired from teaching and Marie is 85. I have memorized the long form, what they call the one-hundred-and-eight, but the truth is I am only going through the motions. I haven't even learned to breathe like a baby. "Soft on the outside, hard on the inside," Tom tells us. "Move like a willow." We are learning to feel our balance, letting strength come not from muscles but from ligaments and tendons and bones and central equilibrium. And then, eventually, from something deeper than bone. "Establish a root," he tells us. "Use the earth." T'ai Chi takes five lifetimes to learn, he says. Everything else is still a mystery to me, but that much I think I understand.

Art Appreciation

All the old Wasco baskets are owned by museums. Most of us in the room tonight knew that, if only because we had read the newspaper story that had brought us here. But how could we know what it meant when, in a locked room off limits to most visitors, a Wasco woman had been allowed to break the plastic seal and feel the smell of camas root rise up strong, surrounding her in that sterile air? It was a long way from home, that nineteenth century basket still wearing its memory of Oregon camas in the heart of New York City. The woman had smiled as she told this story. "Look," she was saying now, pointing to another slide. "See these mothers with the babies inside them? Their hearts lean left, slightly off center. And these? Not butterflies, but condors—common in the Gorge then. Can you find the giant condor, this dim ghost behind the weave?"

It was late winter, a February night. Dean and I had driven east of Pendleton to the old St. Andrew's Mission, huddled against the shadow of the Blue Mountains where jagged chunks of ice still rose like breastworks against our snow tires in the long gravel drive. Crow's Shadow Institute of the Arts, founded by Walla Walla tribal artist James Lavadour, occupies the very building where the Indian boarding school once held its students. Tonight's program had attracted two distinct audiences—Indian people and non-Indian patrons of the arts—to hear Wasco weaver Pat Courtney Gold report on her recent trip to New York. Funded by a grant, she had visited the museums where the Wasco baskets have been preserved for decades. It was important that she make this journey, she explained, because none of the old baskets had survived on the reservation. And no one at home remembered how to make the old designs. She had wanted to bring them back—in her mind, her heart, her fingers—and teach them to other weavers. Tonight she was showing pictures of the baskets she had found. And she hoped to inspire others to follow in her footsteps, make journeys of their own to these New York museums. She had discovered other Plateau peoples' older baskets there too, she said. Cayuse, Walla Walla, Umatilla wisdom. Nimiipu.

Now she was shaking her head at the joke: latex gloves, on fingers that can remember fibers only by touch. "They didn't want me to taste them, either," she laughed. "See this gold layer? That's canary grass. In one museum, though, they let me touch the baskets. No one else had, for seven decades. I was the first who'd asked to see the Wasco sally bags... Dogbane makes a strong warp, thick as my finger, to bear the weight. These little tufts are cattail down. Do you recognize these? Topknots of quail." The slides changed, illuminating her black T-shirt only briefly. The shirt stretched to her knees, almost like a dress. At first I thought it was covered with stars. It took me a while to realize the design was skyscrapers, the lights of all those windows. "Now here, the weaver has used hop string. And see how she's unraveled blankets for bits of color, red and gold?" The hop string, I knew, was from the hard times when Northwest Indian people had to travel as migrant farm laborers, picking hops and apples. Another slide. "Some of the young women I'm teaching want a perfect cylinder," she said as a long bag filled the screen. "But I ask them to remember that fibers choose their own shapes."

When the lights came up we were sitting in rows like the ridges of rutted ice outside the old brick building, still bundled hard against the cold. We blinked at each other. How could this have happened? *All* the old baskets, all knowledge of the old designs, stored in locked rooms? in a city that felt, to many of us here tonight, beyond reach—years distant from these mountains at our backs, these blue-shadowed walls of fear for the people in the Oregon Trail wagons: *cross them by October, or die...* We stared at the white screen, images still burning in our minds. Women with babies inside them. A sky-circle of condors. I remembered the old Yakama story about Creator giving the first woman "something she could not see or hear or smell or touch," Woman's gifts, something beyond words that she then wove into a basket. I thought of women's hands, cupped at their waists. Baskets held the spring roots (*our little sisters*, someone had told me), and summer's gift of huckleberries. The fruits of women's journeys, the woman-half of what people needed to survive. But the baskets were full of something even when they were hanging on the wall, empty. Maybe this was part of what those long-dead collectors had been trying to buy, I thought. Something that included but was more than the intricate artistry of the designs and the carefully woven shapes. Did they think this mystery could be purchased, and inventoried, displayed on a shelf?

There were people here, I knew, who understood exactly how it happened, why a Wasco woman had to travel to New York City to find a Wasco basket. They know the stories that are not included in our history textbooks. Most of them were sitting on the other side of the aisle; a man and three women had come in after the program started and settled cross-legged on the old hardwood schoolhouse floor to see the slides. On my side were the people who had arrived early, giving themselves time to admire the pair of blue-rimmed trays heaped with strawberries and kiwi slices and pineapple, cheeses and thin-sliced breads. Patrons of the arts, people who buy paintings and write checks to help support Crow's Shadow. In my own lap lay a small bag of note cards—a copy of a Lavadour design and some Patrice Hall-Walters' fiber-optic photographs of Plateau beadwork, each card wrapped in cellophane. Twelve dollars' worth.

I knew why there were no old baskets in Wasco homes. All of us knew, I suppose, though none of us wanted to remember. I felt the walls around me: in this very school, they say, a little Cayuse/Umatilla boy died when someone filled his mouth with lye soap and taped it shut, punishment for speaking the language of his mother. And it was in that era of boarding schools and forced assimilation, the era of the Vanishing American, that wealthy collectors had bought and sealed away the Wasco baskets. Objects of beauty that would now increase in value, since the Wasco girls would grow up away from their families, learning other designs.

No one moved.

But the artist was still smiling, urging others to follow her path. She understood the obstacles: could we really find our way across this country that we share and not be lost forever? All she had to guide the other weavers were the stories from her own journey. She had stayed at a cheap hotel, a place her Merchant Marine husband knew about called The Sailors' Inn, with only two cockroaches shadowing the walls and a friendly staff who showed her where to walk, how to find the subway. "You'll recognize it," she laughed. "It smells like Badger's den." Yes, she urged, even those of us for whom New York City seems too far away from what we know, yes, even we could ride through Wall Street with those men in suits, men who were careful not to touch the dirty one who swayed, eyes closed...he lives below the sun, in dirt-lined shafts that don't connect to any rail lines; she had seen him going off into the darkness, maybe he shares his life with badgers, one of the Badger People . . . and there was music, too, people with violins and tambourines and open guitar cases at every stop—

I was walking along her words, feeling the earth beneath each step (maybe it was possible, I thought, even for me; I too might find my way into the secret spaces of marble, oils, acrylics, fibers, of symphonies and operas; even without the Art Appreciation class I didn't get to take because of all those education courses, even with no knowledge of ballet or fine wines or city transportation; maybe I too could walk through New York City and still somehow find my way home), when the director rose before us in a black dress. It was getting late, she said. She hated to stop tonight's program but she needed to make sure people had time to sample the strawberries and breads and visit with the artist before we left.

Pat stood still. No one moved. Then an Indian woman sitting on the floor in front of the folding chairs said something about the Cockroach People and laughed, and we all got up, gathering our coats tighter around us and pulling on hats and gloves.

Outside, Dean and I walked the length of the brick-walled building on the way back to our car. "Why did they stop her? Didn't they understand what she was doing?" His voice was strangled, small. I reached for his hand. Who knows the language for such things? The school was a dark shape above us. It's different now, I told myself. People admire Father Mike; the old St. Andrews Church now honors Indian regalia, the kind people were once commanded to burn. Pardon has been asked for the deep hurts of this place, and people have tried hard to forgive. And now this mission school, where little boys rose at 4 a.m. to drill in military formation in the snow (rough and tough, hard to bluff) is Crow's Shadow, now it's a good thing. A brilliant Indian artist providing classes and equipment and workshops to help other artists, especially Native artists, learn both traditional and non-traditional art forms, and how to market them too. It's important, that side of it. Isn't it? People still have to eat. And Pat Courtney Gold had said weavers surround her now. They circle her like planets, women of all ages hungry for this meal, learning the secrets of the old grasses, bringing back the old designs and creating new ones.

But none of my arguments stopped the thought that kept pushing its way through: what if I had been a teacher in those days, instead of now?

The Old Emigrant Hill road dipped back down onto dry pavement as it headed toward the freeway. In the moonlight just beyond the river's cottonwoods rose Tamastslikt Cultural Institute, its many-angled roof reflecting the shape of the folding foothills just above it, those open slopes where in early spring biscuit root would once more spread its yellow promise across the shallow, rocky soil. Tamastslikt—"to interpret," or as one elder told me, "to turn around"—considers the Oregon Trail from the point of view of the people who looked up at those descending wheels. I remembered the trail's sesquicentennial anniversary in 1993, when mounted warriors rode up the hill to challenge the foot soldiers of this invasion who walked beside the re-enactment wagons. Then, of course, they took these families them home for dinner, a big salmon feast. But they had hoped to make a point. It would still take hundreds of local contributions and then the money from the new casino to build Tamastslikt. Baker City, on the other side of the Blues, and Oregon City, at the end of the trail, had received all the federal funding when Oregon Trail Interpretive Centers were constructed to guide tourists through this history.

The first time we visited Tamastslikt, Dean and I found our names on one of the many silver salmon leaping along the lobby wall, our $25 contribution memorialized as if we too were wealthy donors. Every salmon was exactly the same size.

I should feel rich tonight, I thought, headed home laden with so many stories to share with my students. "They got terribly excited when I wanted to put the tule duck decoy into the water," Pat had said. "They didn't understand that dry tules welcome water and swell back to life. This ancient duck could have floated again, watertight." The moon rode the horizon, traveling just ahead of us. What's on it, then? A man? A frog, as the Nez Perce say? A flag? From the road's edge, the winter-dormant grasses leaned into my headlights, weaving their own patterns across tonight's visions, lines of red and gold. And that smell of camas root, as strong as if the basket were still used every spring.

But I kept remembering the artist as she stood there in that long moment of silence, her eyes still full of stories. Maybe she was wondering if we had seen enough. Or maybe she was wondering which stories we could hear. *Badger People*, I found myself thinking. *Cockroach People. People.*

Getting Dressed

At first I thought getting dressed was a problem I could solve. I drew a picture—arms and legs, what today would be recognizable as toddler coveralls. "That's what I want to wear," I told my mother. Red, I added. Had I seen them somewhere? I'm not sure children had coveralls in 1948, but I remember the joy of imagining something so comfortable.

At home my sister and I wore baggy blue jeans—there's a picture of me in the swing our father had made for us, the jeans' cuffs rolled up at least twice to make them fit my short legs—and they weren't bad either. But when we went to visit our grandparents on Sundays Jill and I had to wear the ruffle-scratchy, look-alike dresses we had inherited from our cousins. They tied at the waist, in the back. Red corduroy coveralls, I thought, were the obvious solution. But they never appeared in the hand-me-down boxes, and although Mom said she thought I'd had a great idea, what she made on her sewing machine for my first day of school a few years later was a plaid gingham dress. Except for the seam that rubbed the back of my neck, it wasn't so scratchy. And it smelled new, just like my two-layer box of sixteen sharp crayons and my Buster Brown oxfords. Still, it was definitely a dress.

In the first grade class photo, though, I'm wearing my size 6X blue jeans with the button-on suspenders and that red pullover sweater. Mom had let me wear my favorite outfit for three days in a row. I am in the top row and my smile is enormous: those jeans and that pullover were as close as my wardrobe could come to letting people know that I was actually a cowboy.

Not everyone approved of my tastes. My sister was embarrassed. "Oh, Bette, those jeans!" she scolded one chilly morning a few years later as we waited beneath the fir tree for the school bus. Jill was a seventh grader now—stunning, I thought, in her fitted blue coat with its imitation fur-trimmed yoke; once I reached junior high, and all through high school, I too would have to wear dresses, except on Fridays. But that was still two years away. My own winter coat was my older cousin Larry's black-checkered mackinaw, the best thing I had ever found in the used clothing boxes unless I counted his yellow shirt.

For now, Mom let me dress the way I wanted to—that year, my start of school outfit had been a blue corduroy shirt of my very own, and Wrangler jeans—but on Christmas morning the year I was in sixth grade and sliding into puberty there was no much-anticipated crystal radio kit under the tree. My package felt squishy. Beneath the Christmas wrapping lay a soft white eyelet blouse and black taffeta skirt with a sequined butterfly. It was as close as my mother could come to the poodle skirt all the girls wanted that year. All the girls but one.

When the mandatory dress-code years descended, she assured me that shirtwaist dresses would work just fine for the noon basketball games on the playground—my friend Connie and I were still invited to join in—but I was worried. Dribbling was tricky, even without the half-slip that made the other girls' skirts stick out like hoops, layers and layers of stiff nylon mesh. My legs could move freely, though, almost as fast as the boys', and we all came in for our one o'clock math class looking pretty much the same, red-faced and sweaty in the late September heat. I knew this kind of thing wouldn't be allowed much longer. That was the worst part of this dressing business: the feeling that my real self was all wrong.

Then came high school. Algebra, amazing tricks with numbers, and finally even the literature books I had been waiting for so long, but high school also meant new worries about clothes. There was so much more to getting dressed now than feeling comfortable or staying warm, and it was all big stuff, important stuff, about becoming women. It seemed to be going smoothly enough for the other girls—even though they anguished about boys and hair, they knew what to wear—but I was spectacularly unsuccessful. Part of the problem was money, or lack of it, something that hadn't mattered so much when I could just wear jeans. We were better off than my mother had been when she had to wear a neighbor's cast-off high heels to attend seventh grade, and Mom didn't have to cut down Dad's old shirts to make our blouses any more. And our father worked extra shifts at the mill in August—his check stub read "vacation pay"—to help with school expenses. But there wasn't enough money to buy what the other girls were wearing. Jill and I each had $30 to spend. She chose burgundy and camel-colored winter fabrics from the Sears catalog, and she looked so petite and graceful in the V-necked burgundy jumper that was in style that year and the straight camel skirt with its matching fitted vest. Since she had waited until after the first week of school to order her new shoes, she wore the same low-cut saddle shoes that the other girls somehow already knew would be in style that September. But I'd had to spend $16 of my funds on the support bras my new figure required, and the pleated blue plaid skirt Mom made didn't make me look at all like the girls in those slim stitched-down pleats who floated past me in the halls. My saddle shoes were the same big clunky kind they had left behind in sixth grade.

When the lumber industry began to falter and I knew the mill would slow or even shut down during the winter months, I resolved to buy my own clothes. If I had any hope of making it to college I had to save every penny of my 4-H money, but I could spare the ribbon award check that would arrive in the mail after the late-September fair, and maybe part of my egg money. Besides, last year's skirts still fit, so I didn't really need much, and by now I had pretty much given up any attempt to be a well-dressed, socially acceptable kind of girl: there had to be more to becoming a woman than following the fashions. But my clothing problems didn't go away. I took catalog descriptions too literally: the trench coat with its thin ("toasty") zip-out liner nearly let me freeze on the countless mornings when the school bus arrived not only late but with a broken heater. And sometimes, of course, it was impossible not to care. Steve asked me to the winter Snow Ball two days before the dance; not nearly enough time, Mom agreed, to buy fabric and make a formal, and of course buying a dress was out of the question. When I met Steve in the empty history classroom, both of us were rigid with embarrassment.

"I'm sorry, I can't go. I don't have a formal, I thought maybe my mom could—but she says there isn't time…"

Steve's face was as red as mine. "Oh," he said.

"I can't just buy one. Mom would have to make it because—"

"Oh," Steve said again.

"I'm sorry."

"No, no. It's okay."

Did he have any idea what I was talking about? My tongue felt like a wedge of cheese. It could not find the words to say *Of all the boys in our class, Steve, you are the one I would like to date. You're smart and kind and I love the way your eyes crinkle at the edges when you laugh. I have wanted to walk beside you, let you know that someone sees you. And I have imagined that you would see me walking there and realize that you liked me too. Now here we are, standing here alone in front of Miss Bradbury's desk and I can't even explain that my family is too poor to buy the right kind of dress for this dance, barely able to afford the fabric to make a homemade version, and you asked me so late that there just isn't time for that.*

I had friends, and I liked school. But my problem with clothes followed me like a shadow. In my junior year when the spring music festival was held at the university in Moscow, I had played first trumpet in a band that had just been awarded a number one rating, and the lilacs were in bloom. We were on our way down to the Student Union Building when two seniors, Melinda and Laura, beckoned me into the back seat of Laura's car. Laura had already invited me to be the editor of next year's student newspaper, the position she held now. They both admired me, Melinda said. I had so much potential. All I had to do was dress a bit better... I could do that, couldn't I?

⤚⭢⬥⭢○⭠⬥⭠⤙

I have never owned a pair of red corduroy coveralls and I've lost the suspenders, but anyone who knew me as a child could probably have predicted what I wear most days. Miracle of miracles, I have even lived to see the era of women wearing blue jeans to work. Though I read recently that young women are having toes amputated so their feet will fit into the latest Hollywood-inspired footwear, I know I'm not the only woman I know who considers Birkenstocks dress shoes.

But getting dressed can still be a problem. Something lurks at the back of my closet, whispering *wrong, wrong, wrong*.

I was amazed to learn, when we talked about this as adults, that my sister had heard the same voice all through high school. ("That awful burgundy jumper?" she said. "You thought ...!") But I probably should not have been surprised. Even the popular, more affluent girls must have felt this pressure. They may even have felt it most keenly. Sometimes I wonder, as I walk by the upscale women's clothing store in our town and glance at the fashions draped over the mannequins in the windows, about the people who shop here at Malarkey's. Were they the girls who wore purple tights in second grade so everyone could tell at a glance that they were really ballerinas? I smile, hoping this long-draped silken skirt is exactly who they are now.

When I left high school for the University of Idaho, where men could wear anything and often did—one showed up in his low-cut swim briefs to listen to a lecture on Melville—women still had to wear skirts or dresses except to breakfast and Saturday lunch, or when we were inside our dorm rooms. Winters are cold on the Palouse prairie, but there was no respite even when we circumvented the rules by walking to town or sneaking into the library in "cutoffs," jeans hemmed just above our knees and hidden under our carefully buttoned (but still chilly) trench coats. Before I left for my student teaching assignment in another town even farther north, Professor Banks called me into his office and wished me well, encouraging me to wear things like the turquoise sweater and brown/turquoise plaid skirt I happened to have on, the same skirt and sweater I had been wearing that day in the back seat of Laura's car. The sweater had frayed a bit more in four years. "Kids appreciate bright colors," he said. He could hardly wait to hear how I liked teaching. I remembered the other time he had invited Eugenie and me to his office—just after our invitations to join Phi Beta Kappa had arrived in the campus mail. "Now this is a good thing, you'll want to do this," he told us. "And if you don't happen to have the twenty-five dollar membership fee, I do."

Eugenie and I walked together from the moldy Castle Court Motel to our first teaching assignments, teetering on the December ice in the high heels required by the Education Department "so students will know you are a teacher." A few weeks into the term I tried to visit her junior high classroom, but the hall monitor leaned over the stairwell to shout down at me: "Get right back out that door! All students outside during noon break!" The shoes were not working their magic, apparently. Later in the term, as I was getting up from my teacher's desk to answer a student's question about the poems we were writing that day, I forgot that the desk's lower drawer was open. Allison was a quiet fifteen, but she brought me extra assignments every day, a writer's journal. Good, good stuff. "Oh, Allie, you're off to a good start here. Now you just need to—Crash. Through Allison's outstretched arms to the tiled floor at her feet. Head over high heels.

"Oh!" said Allie, turning red. "Oh Miss Lynch, I'm so sorry!"

The following year, in my own first high school classroom, my biggest clothing problem turned out to be nylons. For a long time I didn't allow myself to buy panty hose because I just couldn't afford to replace both legs every time one snagged on my splintery desk. I lived in the back of Harold's General Merchandise, so every afternoon, after I had kicked my way out of the pinching "flats" and let the skirt fall in a heap I could step out of, breathing deeply for the first time all day, I headed around the corner to pick up my mail—Harold was the postmaster as well as provider of groceries, coveralls, and snow shovels—say hello to my landlord, and purchase tonight's can of soup and tomorrow's pair of nylons.

A few years later I would campaign for women's right to wear pantsuits at a Montana middle school. I had bought the first one I'd seen in a Missoula store window, lime green with white sleeves and a sash that tied. My principal thought it was deplorable, and it was. But it was a suit, an ensemble dressy enough for a seventh grade English classroom, I argued. There was no reason why women teachers couldn't simply wear slacks and blouses, for that matter, since many of the men wore slacks and shirts but no jacket or tie. I had accepted a teaching job in Oregon for the coming year, so the principal just sighed and waited for me to move along. He already had his hands full enforcing the students' dress code: girls could wear jeans as long as they were any color but blue, and boys could wear T-shirts as long as they were any color but white. If girls wore blue jeans, he had explained, they would not grow up to be good mothers.

By the time the next criticism of the way I dressed appeared on my teaching evaluation, I had become a mother and was doing my level best to imitate the styles I studied carefully in the faculty lounge, 1970s-era polyester slacks and blouses with sashes that looped into bows under my chin. Dean said I was beautiful in the fitted leather jacket that tied at the waist. The principal wouldn't explain why he had checked *Needs Improvement*, but he reassured me that he already knew I would try to do better next year.

Only once had my clothes been absolutely right. In 1970, when I enrolled in the University of Colorado graduate school of English, everybody in Boulder—or at last the twenty thousand students and an equally large number of hippie "street kids" that fall—wore blue chambray work shirts. My dad had given me one of his just before I left. It didn't fit quite right, he said, but it was brand new, and he thought maybe I could use it. Sometimes, as we gathered under the golden-leafed chestnut trees next to guitar and flute players, looking up when the Hari Krishnas sang their way past us—we had class on the lawn every time there was a war-protest bomb threat—I wondered if I were the only student here whose father actually wore a chambray shirt to work every day. The shirt fit me perfectly.

➤┼◆➤━O━◄➤┼◄

"Time to retire this one, honey. Why not get yourself a new blue sweater?" We have been married for over three decades, so Dean knows exactly how long it has taken me to allow myself to spend money on clothes. His support helped me make that leap—and thanks to his amazing laundry skills, everything I own is not permanently stained with tomatoes, either.

But his gentle nudges are mixed blessings. If there is a personal hell for each of us, mine will be a shopping mall.

Last summer, sitting around a picnic table under the midnight stars with two women writing friends—we were trying to decide what to wear to an unexpected reading we had been invited to give to a local women's group—I confessed to the voice that still lurks in my closet. Partly, I told them, it's my still-leaning-toward-tomboy tastes, but there's more to it, too. Somehow I'm not sure that I'll be dressed appropriately, or even what appropriately means. It's still hard to let myself spend money on clothes, especially on styles and fabrics I don't really like. But then, of course, I'm unprepared. And even as an adult I have let myself be shamed into missing some event I wanted to attend—the Santa Fe Opera, for instance—because someone suggested that I didn't have the right clothes. After some laughter and mutual sharing, one of the women asked, "Do you have any objection to getting a box of used clothing in the mail?"

"Well, no," I said. "Of course not." I pictured the yellow shirt coming out of the box once again, that black-checkered mackinaw...

She must have had second thoughts, though, because the box never arrived. Just as well, since I had been having second thoughts myself.

"I've got to buy something nice," I tell Dean. "Just have the thing, whatever it is, hanging in the closet. Like everybody else." He nods. He has heard this before. And it's not, he knows, that I haven't tried.

Last year I published my first book. That meant bookstore readings, but I had new khakis, and a friend had bolstered me through a series of "let's get out of here" moments in a crowded shopping center long enough to help me pick out a pair of comfortable leather shoes that I could tolerate without my orthotic inserts. I was set, right? Unless, as Dean kept kidding, I got invited to be on Oprah. Then a package arrived from my Aunt Carolyn. "I thought about sending flowers, but decided you'd like this instead," read the card. I pushed aside white tissue paper and lifted out a blue-checkered jacket. "She's trying to dress me for the readings, isn't she?" I asked Dean. "That's the plan," he grinned. They had been talking.

So I walked into Malarkey's and bought a pair of black slacks. I had to struggle through the proprietor's offerings, three pairs of split-waistband velveteen pull-ons, to get to the tailored pair, and I didn't look at the price tag until I was at the counter. That seemed to be the secret of this kind of shopping. "How long have you lived here?" the woman asked as she wrapped the slacks in tissue. "I don't think I've seen you before."

"Fifteen years," I told her.

The black slacks are soft and lovely, and the woman at Tiny Tailor has hemmed them to exactly the right length. I felt good at my first reading. Good, but not quite myself. For some reason I kept remembering the description that a good friend had given her son when he came to meet me in a crowded airport: "Look for a small woman with short white hair. She'll be wearing blue jeans and looking as if she'll take no prisoners." The young man said he wasn't so sure about the take-no-prisoners part, but he had no trouble locating me.

For the next reading, I was already thinking, I'll just slip into a pair of khakis. Or maybe that new pair of Land's End blue jeans.

Bette Lynch Husted

Hope, for the Dry Side

The truth is, I am trying to change things. Transfiguration, that's what I'm aiming at—nothing less. "I'm not going to be a writer," some of my students say when I push them too far. "You already are," I tell them. "That's what you're doing here, writing." I know what they mean, of course.

Jerry has a pretty good idea what I'm up to, he says, slamming his book shut. "This college has an agenda." His voice is just a little too loud. My heart jumps, but I like the way he looks me in the eye. Only three days into the term, and I have already noticed his quick mind, the easy kidding way he has with students half his age. "I'm sick of it. I didn't sign up for this." He crosses his arms and pushes back in the too-small desk.

Class hasn't even begun—I have just hurried across campus from my nine o'clock and I'm still unpacking my book bag. But my plan was to discuss Judith Barrington's "Poetry and Prejudice," an essay whose setting is a small town in the Blue Mountains that rise above Pendleton, the mountains our college is named for. Close to us, and painfully close for me, since I once taught in a high school only six miles away from the classroom where Barrington was working as a visiting poet when a boy she calls Brad stood up to read his poem. Write about a moment of decision, she had told them. Brad's poem described the moment when he had accepted his mission in life: to find gays, hunt them down.

Good writing, I had planned to tell my class today, makes you think. When I read Barrington's essay in *The Stories That Shape Us*—the anthology we're using now in class—I went around showing it to people, or leaving copies in their mailboxes. Yet I had felt the shadow of defensiveness, too. "You were in no danger," I told Judith when I took a writing workshop from her that summer. "Brad wouldn't really have followed you back to your cabin with his deer rifle." I was sure of this, in spite of the fact that the class she had been teaching had dissolved into laughter at Brad's poem. I didn't know Brad, but nothing like this had ever happened when Judith visited my own classroom as a poet-in-the-school, and Brad was probably just like my students—capable of cruel jokes about subjects they found frightening, yes, but not of murder.

Yet I kept thinking about Michelle. She had been my sister's longtime friend, so I clipped the developing story from Oregon newspapers as the facts about her disappearance became clear, and the facts were that Michelle and her partner had been bound with duct tape and shot in the head, their bodies stuffed into the canopy of their little pickup until someone noticed the smell, because they were lesbians. I wanted to tell my students how I had finally decided that at some deep level Judith was right to call attention to the connections between prejudice and violence and guns, even if people in our communities carry rifles the same way they carry flashlights and spare tires, and even if I could still hope I was right about Brad.

And even if, when I heard her read the essay, I felt tears rise. For Judith's courageous and graceful words, yes, and for the image of her returning to the high mountain valley to read them aloud in the very place where she had hesitated to speak before—but mostly, I wanted to admit to my students, because I could hear the audience around me whispering *yes, I know what she means, that's how those people are.*

Is that how we are? Are rural people really this lost, this hopeless? That is not what the essay says, but it's what the audience seemed to have heard. I remembered how horrified we had been when the story reached us one morning in the high school teachers' room that the owner of a local motel had refused to let an African-American woman spend the night. But other than shake our heads and feel sick, what had we done about it? Maybe we had further to go than I wanted to admit. I wasn't innocent, either: the first time she taught in our school, Judith had sought my advice before an upcoming reading at the local bookstore—would there be repercussions if she read certain poems? Students were planning to attend. It was the same concern that would later prompt her silence after Brad read his poem. I had told her yes, reading poems in which she referred to being gay might lead to problems—I too was worried that she might not be invited back to our school. What could I have done differently? Could I have said don't worry, if there are repercussions I'll help defuse them? Or could I have been braver still, brave enough to believe in the very hope I would later defend so stubbornly—that the people in my community were not people she needed to fear? The point is, I had planned to tell my class as we looked closely at the structure and scenes and the way she weaves the images, this is an example of where I want you to go in your own essays. I want your essays to challenge me, I want you to change my life, the way this one did, and does. So do all your other readers, whether they know it or not.

But no one will be able to hear these things with Jerry's words still hanging in the space between our desks.

"I know the subject matter of this essay might be difficult for some of you." I look around the circle of faces, making eye contact that would have cinched an A in my long-ago Student Teaching practicum. "But I *do* assume that you don't think gays and lesbians, or anyone else, should be hunted down and murdered. As writers, we can all learn from this essay. How can we approach topics we know many of our readers won't have direct experience with? How can we get them to think about things they don't want to have to think about?" No one says anything. Jerry has caught himself, pulled himself back into his student posture, but he's cocking his head, ready for an hour's argument. Or a term's, I think. "And of course everyone's been in the narrator's shoes in one way or other." I'm talking faster than I usually do. "Think of all the times you've known what you should have done, what was the morally right thing to do, but were afraid to do it—and how that haunted you. Maybe, like Judith Barrington, you were afraid to speak out. Haven't we all lain awake at night replaying the scene, what we should have said? Barrington's essay shows us a model, how the act of writing itself becomes the moment of decision, the moment of moral courage."

All the time I'm talking I am thinking of Judith sitting on her tall stool in that high school classroom, lecturing the kids about statistics and gay teen suicide. Nobody's buying my little speech, either. I doubt if anyone else thinks the college has an agenda, but it would take a pretty dense student not to know that I do. I'm trying to help us all see whole new possibilities, like the tilting circle of the world spreading below you when you stand braced in the wind on top of Eagle Cap. But I am not off to a very good start.

And then Aaron, a farm kid sitting shoulder to shoulder with Jerry and looking all of sixteen with his sun-bleached hair and smudged glasses, says, "I think it's important. I know a lot of gay students here at BMCC who are just plain scared." I can feel other students exhaling, arms shifting slightly on desktops. A woman to my right nods slightly. "This story could have happened in my home town, too," Aaron says. "I'm glad you assigned it."

I will lose Jerry. He hasn't actually read the essay—he's been out of town helping with a youth wrestling tournament all weekend—and he agrees it is only fair that he save his comments until Wednesday. But on Wednesday he is waiting outside the door with a class withdrawal slip. If he changes his mind on this issue, he explains to another teacher, everything he's taught his children means nothing. Then he laughs. Actually, he says, his grown children already disagree with him. "Dad, you're just plain wrong," his daughter tells him.

I pass him in the hall, and we say hello to each other, embarrassed. We both know we could have done better, but neither of us quite knows how.

With teaching, though, you always get another chance. "How can I write about racism?" Angela wants to know when we begin the next essay. "I've never been around it. Everybody in my town is white." *First, do no harm.* "Let's see what you've got so far," I say. "Let's hear your first draft."

Who am I, I keep wondering, to teach about racism? What do I know? I startle them—and myself—with my confession that in the film we have watched together the man I identify with most is the one who keeps saying, "I'm not racist, some of my best friends are the Mexican people who worked in my vineyard, but why are you blocking your own progress? Why can't you just be Americans?" Of course this man is maddeningly obtuse, I tell their staring faces, but I know I must be, too. What am I missing? Am I hurting someone right now with my own inexcusable ignorance? It's so deeply ingrained in our culture—not just racism, but our unconscious acceptance of it—that we have all swallowed it whole.

Joy Harjo told Bill Moyers that she hadn't experienced direct and personal racism except in La Grande, where people threw rocks at the troupe of young Indian actors as they walked down the street. My students think I'm making this up. She must have imagined it. La Grande is 50 miles away, just over Cabbage Hill; it's where they'll go to get their bachelor's degrees at Eastern Oregon University. They learned about multi-culturalism in high school, they say. They're horrified by the video that shows Emmett Till in his coffin but that was in the *Fifties*. Things are different now, Cami says. I tell them about Mary, my student from Joseph who married a black man and took on the name of Hope, and how her father—who taught her to judge a person only by action—has refused to answer her letters or meet his gifted and beautiful grandchildren, who are now seven and nine years old. Their school pictures bloom like blanket flowers on my refrigerator door. I look at their eyes and remember their mother, how she skipped the senior class trip and waited in the dark classroom to surprise me when I turned on the light. She and her friend Sandy, the Chief Joseph Days rodeo princess. Neither of them wanted to miss the last mythology class.

I don't tell them all that, of course, or how I found Grace Paley's story "Traveling" in the *New Yorker* and sent it to Mary Hope, and how she sent a copy to her father, and how he responded with that deep silence. The story tells of a train ride when Paley, holding a tired African-American woman's sleeping child, had opened her eyes to a white man's loud voice: "Lady, I wouldn't of touched that thing with a meat hook." I don't tell them, either, about Mary's letter to the *Wallowa County Chieftain* when the Enterprise school board was trying, unsuccessfully at first, to change its "Savages" mascot. Even I was surprised when she told her family story in the small town newspaper. How do you measure a wife's love—and a mother's—against a daughter's? When do you decide the only way to talk with your father about racism is in the county paper?

But I do tell them how, when Evangelina wrote that a fellow BMCC student had come up to her in the hallway and said, "What are you doing here, Beaner? You'll never make it—get back in the fields where you belong," I was astonished. I felt my mouth hanging open like the entrance to an underground cave. I must have looked a lot like the man in our film.

Change happens, but it's hard. It's exhausting. Sean writes about his shame over his first draft, a flimsy story he made up to get a grade rather than tell the truth about his childhood. It was too embarrassing, he said, to admit the overt racism in his family; he had risked his father's beatings every time he walked home with his African-American friends. Cami had visited in the elevator with three good-looking high school boys—football stars, honor students, who turned out to be the defendants at the white supremacy murder trail in the Phoenix office building where she had volunteered during spring break. "I don't know why I thought racism was something that happened a long time ago," she said. "This wasn't in the Fifties. This was a month ago." Angela's third draft describes her reaction to James's essay. "I was ashamed," she tells me during our conference. "When he talked about how that woman took her kids out of the pool when his Tribal Recreation Program kids lined up to go in, my first reaction was to look for some other reason, to justify." Evangelina finds the courage to read her paper aloud. Lucy does too. We hear about the Kopper Kitchen waitress who wouldn't serve her Native family, and the owner of the high school lunch hangout who grabbed her by the wrist and dragged her through the crowd to the counter, where the clerk verified that yes, she actually had paid for her Nachos. "When the black man got mad and yelled at the white man in that film, I wanted to stand up and cheer," she writes. "But I was looking for another brown face, someone safe to sit beside. I could hear people all around me getting mad." It's the mountains that sustain her, she says. This ancient, guiding land where she belongs. Tears stream down her face. "I don't understand," she tells me after class. "I read it to my daughter this morning and wasn't upset at all." Her daughter, who comes to class with Lucy on her school's parent-teacher conference days, is eight years old.

I should be happy, I tell myself. Luke, who is repeating the class—he'd had a hard time with the racism assignment the first time around—writes a mystical story that links a hunting trip with family beliefs about the Ku Klux Klan in a way that will continue to haunt me for years. I am so proud of him I feel like his mother. But for many students the term ends too soon. Aaron has started to tell us about his Cherokee ancestor who was rescued from the Trail of Tears, her life saved at the cost of her identity. Years later, when this woman's brother comes to her home, she says, "I don't know you," and buries the cup he has drunk from in the back yard. But what Aaron has turned in is the ragged half of a first draft. "I'm sorry," he says. "It's been quite a week. My mother has been in the hospital since Tuesday. We've been taking turns sitting with her, and I haven't had much sleep." Aaron, the boy who saved the class for us all, hasn't learned to write. I want to give him a B for Beauty but he'd flounder in Writing 123. I want to hug him, and I do.

Has anyone really changed? Have I? What I will take home with me for the summer is Mark. Like Jerry, Mark is a bright older student, deeply grateful to be in college at last. After three conferences and five drafts, what he has is an argument that there is a difference between racism and intelligent discrimination: a tortured defense of his right to "choose." When he reads it aloud on the last day, I look down at my desk. It's long.

After class he stands in the doorway, waiting for me. "I don't feel good about my writing," he says. "I'm not at all satisfied with the work I've done."

"Promise me," I tell him, "that you'll keep writing for the rest of your life." He's a quiet man who doesn't smile much. Maybe I wouldn't either, if I were raising an inherited family and working until midnight every night at the mill, after an 8 - 4 day at school. We both know he's the best writer in the class, and we both know we need to do better.

When school is over I drive west to a women's writing conference, where I will take a class called "Storytelling" from Grace Paley. After a lifetime of fighting for civil rights and women, someone asks her—and after working so long to end war—when you hear the news, how do you keep from becoming pessimistic? "Oh, if I catch myself feeling a little low," she answers, "it's because I'm in a period where I'm not doing much. Hope is one thing only: hope is action." She looks directly at us. "When I'm working, I feel hopeful," she says.

"Now I want to read you something." She has so many stories to tell: which will she choose? "It's called 'Traveling.'" My eyes close, but there is no blocking these tears. They rise like the river outside the room where we listen, the river whose source is all those underground springs in the dark mountains above us.

I write this remembrance more than fifty years later, I hear Grace Paley's voice. I look back at that mother and child. I see how young she is. Her hand on his head is quite small, though she tries by spreading her fingers wide to hide him from the white man. But the child I'm holding, his little face as he turns toward me, is the dark-brown face of my own grandchild, my daughter's boy, the open mouth of the sleeper, the full lips, the thick little body of a child who runs wildly from one end of the yard to the other, leaps from dangerous heights with experienced caution, muscling his body, his mind, for coming realities.

The story circles around my body. If it were a lake I could breathe it.

When her voice stops I step outside into the rush of cool air and the sound of whitewater. I'm thinking about my students, my neighbors on both sides of these mountains. Human beings live here at the edge of the wilderness with me, I know. But we're none of us quite as human as we could be. How many of us are ready to get down on our hands and knees—an Indian custom Grace demonstrated for us in class today—and paint a welcome on our doorstep to all who enter our lives? It's Juneteenth, so much light in the evening sky it seems this day will never stop. Yet I know it's almost time to go home and try again.

Jointly

It's two a.m. The shaft of light from the hospital hallway is dim, but I can make out a reflection in the chrome-polished steel ball. The ball is smaller than I had imagined it would be, and heavier. And warm; I have been gripping it all night, ever since the surgeon held it out toward us in the family waiting area and I reached through a circle of shoulders—my sister and brothers' arms were hanging, stunned, at their sides—to accept it. He had just removed it from our mother's right hip. For 25 years, since her first Total Hip Replacement the year she was 59, this steel ball has held her up. She has walked up mountain trails, carried her grandchildren, stood to accept awards at work. The short stem at the base of the ball is jagged, like the great splinter that sometimes sticks up from a stump, that sawyer's hinge that can rip from a tree if it falls a bit too soon and twists slightly off course. It had taken him more than two hours to cut through the stem, the doctor told us. He looked tired. "It didn't make me happy to do this," he said.

Hip joint: ball and socket. Who will she be, I wonder, when she opens her eyes tomorrow morning, this woman without a hip joint to connect her right leg to her body? My mother, of course. My mom. The red number that measures her oxygen level stumbles along the edge of danger: 89, 88, 87. If it gets down to 85, it means her body is forgetting to breathe. I look down. The dim image at the center of the polished ball is curved and distorted, like the reflections in shoplifting-prevention mirrors that wedge into high corners of late-night convenience stores. When I bend closer, the face blurs to a shapeless ghost in the center of my palm.

Jointly. Such a long time ago, the day when I learned that word. Or began to learn it. Maybe this is what it really meant, then? Is this what it has taken to make me finally understand? My fingers close again around the warm steel ball. I hold my breath, listening for the sound that means my mother is still breathing.

>-┼-◆>-◆-O-◆┼-◆┼-<

It didn't make sense, but I wrote the word on my paper anyway. I hated these assignments, hated even the smell of these new books we had to be so careful with. Pages of exercises to make your hand sore from writing at the end of the school day, and what did they have to do with spelling? This time we were supposed to add "ly," make the words on this week's spelling list into adverbs. Joint plus ly, jointly. Like a joint? Elbowly? I had never heard anyone use such a word. In the manner of knee? Wrist-like? I couldn't make it make sense. "Like an elbow," I wrote, finally. Then I folded the paper inside the spelling book and raised the desk lid. Pages of long division to take home tonight, as usual. Other desks were going up too; an end of the school day whispering rustled behind these shelters. Fifteen more minutes. Then the dismissal bell would ring, and then I'd have the bus ride home and the long night ahead. My brothers had been sick ever since Monte had his smallpox vaccination. They had big red circles all over their little backs and bellies, and high fevers. It seemed as if they'd been sick forever.

Mrs. Markle was getting angry. Too much noise. If we were through this early, we must not have done the assignment, she said. No, Barbara protested. We're finished. "We'll see," said Mrs. Markle. "Bette, define 'jointly.'"

"I didn't understand that one," I said. People turned in their desks and looked back at me. Now was not the time to let them down. "I wrote 'like an elbow,' but I don't think that's right."

"I thought so," said Mrs. Markle. "There will be an extra spelling assignment tonight. Everyone will write each spelling word fifteen times—and, do Exercise C on page 44." She walked back to her desk. Her cheeks were always red, she used that kind of makeup, but now they were brighter.

"But we did the assignment!" said Barbara. "Lots of people know the answer!"

"Is that so?" said Mrs. Markle. Hands shot up: Jim, Lanny, Connie, a half dozen others. Everybody but me, it seemed, knew what jointly meant. They were trying to sit especially straight; Mrs. Markle often dismissed us by rows, the Boy Scout row going first on Wednesdays when they had their uniforms on and all of them put their hands together prayer style on their desks. Finally she called on Roy, who didn't have his hand up. Then David, who had been staring at the back of Judy's head, a dead giveaway that he didn't know either. All around the room arms were lifting higher, straighter. "Linda," said Mrs. Markle. "What does 'jointly' mean?"

Connie gasped. Linda would have been in Special Ed. if Special Ed. had been part of our lives then; she had been passed along to sixth grade with us but she couldn't read. "I don't know," said Linda. She was looking at the floor. Her face was as red as mine felt. Was blood beating in her ears too?

"Jointly': doing something together. Two students might work jointly to check their math homework, for example," said Mrs. Markle. She walked back to her desk and sat down. "The assignment is due first thing tomorrow morning. If it's not completed there will be serious consequences."

"That's not fair!" said Connie. "Lots of kids had their hands up. And just because Bette almost always knows the answers and she doesn't know this one doesn't mean we should all have extra work. She *did* it! She just didn't understand one thing."

"It will be good for you," said Mrs. Markle. She was still mad, but she was smiling now. She folded her hands above her spiral-bound grade book. What better use could we possibly make of our time this evening? It was the kind of question we weren't supposed to answer.

>-!->-•-<-!-<

Across the hospital corridor an old man is watching television, all three lights at the head of his bed turned to their highest settings. When does he sleep? I can barely make out my mother's face behind the mounded blanket, those wedges of blue foam and footgear holding her in place. Weights hang from a traction bar. Down the hall someone is moaning; the sound rises to a mangled scream. Your mother won't remember this part, the doctor has told us.

On my way down the hill to the hospital at 2 a.m.—family members are taking turns with these bedside vigils, most of my siblings camped at our aunt's house—I had heard a voice on National Public Radio discussing smallpox as a biological weapon. It has been only a year since death crashed out of that blue September morning into what we had thought were the sturdy walls of our cities, New York and Washington, and everyone still feels under attack. Because no one dies of smallpox any more, the experts have begun to realize, we might all die of smallpox. Did this speaker, I wondered, or any of the others who talked about *the homeland*, ever think about Native peoples? Nine out of ten Natives died when smallpox swept across this continent. Smallpox and its allies, measles and influenza. Malaria, scarlet fever. It is Providence—it is the will of God, rejoiced the Puritans. "We are a virgin population," tonight's radio voices had worried aloud. "We have no immunity."

Jointly. Together. I have a sudden image, the kind of visual hallucination that happens when I'm exhausted, of my brother Monte, who had taken the first shift just after the nurses wheeled Mom's bed up from surgery at 9 p.m. He would be in Aunt Carolyn's basement now, sleeping next to his youngest child—a late-life baby just learning to talk. "Chocolate cake," the baby can say, clear as a prayer. "Ee-chee birds"—I see birds. Somewhere near the nation's capital, a sniper has chosen another victim. Is it a terrorist? A serial killer who strikes like lightning, whoever happens to be in front of the rifle sights? School children will be next, the note had warned. "Are there sufficient stores of vaccine?" The radio reception had fuzzed, I remembered, then cleared again as I turned the corner into the hospital parking lot. "Smallpox vaccination, we must remember, is not without risk."

⮞┅◆┅●┅◆┅⮜

You can be thinking about hot chocolate and feeling the day's take of marbles in your pocket, I knew when I was twelve, and suddenly you're in trouble and your stomach is clawing its way up into your heart. It's just the way things are. When I got off the school bus I put the spelling book into the mailbox. Pine needles had just emerged from their snow and dirty gravel blankets, red and slick at the top of the steep driveway. Something in my mouth tasted sharp, like the edge of my jackknife passing a slice of green apple into my mouth. Barbara and Connie and I had made a pact. We wouldn't do the homework.

I knew if I brought the book into the house, though, I would be tempted. I had never left an assignment unfinished. My mistake on "jointly" was only the second time I could remember not knowing the right answer. Hernando de Soto, in fifth grade, that was the other. I had finished the history chapter and was reading *Silver Chief, Dog of the North*. Something about the armored Spanish names of Conquistadors didn't fit on any prairie I could imagine, and when the teacher called my name these syllables had numbed on my tongue. The next time she saw my dad in the aisles of the corner grocery she had told him I was slipping in my studies, reading too many library books.

My little brothers were still crying. I could hear them as I passed the crab apple tree. I laid my math book on the porch and headed out to the woodshed. There would be chickens to feed, supper and dishes and diapers to fold. Mom needed lots of help. We all took turns rocking the boys and bathing them with cool washcloths. But nothing seemed to make them feel any better. Behind the mask of my mother's exhaustion, I could see something else, something that showed only in her eyes.

So I was afraid too.

➤ı◆➤➤◆ı◄

It's called a girdlestone: removing the ball joint from the hip. "This is what we used to do," the surgeon had said, "before we had hip implants. It gives us the best chance to get rid of the infection." He held up the X-ray to show us how the top of the metal implant stem—what used to be femur—will come to rest against scar tissue that will form between it and a muscle, the gluteus medius. "Your leg will be shorter—you'll have to wear a built-up shoe—but it will function without a joint. You'll be able to walk enough to get to the bathroom, move around your room. Beyond that, you will get pretty tired."

Jointly. At the joint, without the joint. Can it be possible? That's exactly what Nazi doctors wanted to know, someone has told me, when they removed the healthy hip joints of prisoners in the concentration camps.

I turn the steel ball in my palm, touching my reflection with the fingers of my other hand. Sometimes I still feel that craving pulling at me. That childhood hunger. I wanted to know everything.

"How did this happen?" my mother will ask me when she awakens. "Why?"

Staphococcus. You may have had the infection for weeks, I could tell her were she not so drugged, were she well enough to listen. Months. Or it might have just happened. The doctor doesn't know. Staphococcus lives on the skin, he says, benignly enough—until you're sick, or weak. I could explain it to her like a story, one she will remember herself when her mind clears: imagine that you have fallen, Mom, in your new apartment at the assisted living center. You're recovering in the hospital, where therapists with names like Justin and Jennifer smile as you walk slowly down the hall and back again. You lean over the walker; muscles spasm in your bad hip. They keep one hand on the belt around your waist, one on your shoulder. "Now don't let that pretty lady run me over!" says a man in house slippers pulling his own physical therapist slowly up the hall. "Don't you give me any trouble!" you grin back at him. And then, as you lie dressed in your sports pants and sweatshirt again, your bags packed for a month of walking therapy in rehab care, a young woman in navy blue scrubs pushes a wheelchair into your room. "We need to take you back upstairs," she says. "The doctor wants to draw some fluid from your hip."

"Do you have the wrong patient?" your daughter asks. "She has been released; we're waiting for the ride to the Care Center."

123

"We just turned back the van at the door," the woman says. "The doctor wants to check something on the X-ray." You climb into the wheelchair, lift an expressive eyebrow at your kids.

And then they're unpacking the plastic bags and you're making choices, impossible choices. However it got there, it's there: raging in the bone and tissue and the old cement leaking from your hip implant. The polished steel hosts a deadly guest. "Girdlestone is definitely indicated," the surgeon says. "But sitting here next to you, a healthy woman—if you were my mother I couldn't tell you to do this." You reach out, touch his shoulder. "That's the trouble with being my age," you say. "Everyone thinks of their mother. It makes it so hard for people."

But how can I tell my mother her own story? How could she believe it?

The sniper has shot a woman this time, someone close to my age. Or it could have been my T'ai Chi teacher's mother, I think, who slumped to the parking lot asphalt at her husband's feet. I met Tom's mother last summer when Tom and Traci's baby was born. She had watched me take the baby from his arms, that small bundle. She was smiling. This time, though, it was someone else, some other woman who also lived near Washington, and it was some other first granddaughter who would arrive too late to be held.

Muscles deteriorate as we grow older, Tom often reminds our T'ai Chi class, but tendons and ligaments can be lengthened and strengthened. Bones can rebuild. Imagine each joint as a pearl, he says. He demonstrates: connect them, thread them together. Move like a string of pearls

▰┅◆┅○┅◆┅▰

The three of us were on our way down the corridor to the principal's office before our class had even stood for the Pledge of Allegiance. A few weeks ago Ormal and Bobby had tried to be manly and gone straight to Mr. Simmons' office when they had accidentally knocked a chip from Mrs. Markle's wooden desk during recess—they were chasing each other, the first time boys had ever flirted this way over me—and they had come back hardly able to walk. How could we have let another busywork assignment get us into this? We'd had dozens, hundreds. But even on our way down that long hallway, we told ourselves that really, we'd had no choice. "It's the principle of the thing," we had agreed after class yesterday afternoon—the same phrase that led to conflicts with marble cheats, playground standoffs that the teachers couldn't understand. "It's just a marble," they said.

I had long since learned not to raise my hand every time I knew the answers, but until sixth grade I had never run into a teacher who disliked me because I knew them. Mrs. Markle tried to hide it, but it was obvious, and it puzzled Connie and Barb as well as me. Now here they were, walking beside me down the long hall to protest my double punishment, for knowledge and for my only lapse in knowing. We were in this together. *Jointly.* Three bones meeting at an elbow. But how could that be, unless the bones stuck out at angles, like jacks...my thoughts wouldn't stay in straight lines. Mr. Simmons' office door was open; he was watching for us. I was shaking.

"What is all this about not doing your assignment?" he said. His white-shirted belly touched the front of his desk and his fingers curled into soft fists. Black hairs bent toward the knuckles. He must be going to yell first..."Mrs. Markle is the best teacher I've got," he told us. "When she says jump, I want you to ask, 'How high?' And that's *all* I want you to ask."

We waited. Was it possible? He was only going to—

"Do you understand me?" Yes. Yes.

Then the sound. Like someone choking. It was Barbara, I finally realized, and she was giggling. She sounded different, though, like when you've been crying so hard you can't catch your breath and you hiccup and cough. Connie stared across me, unable to reach Barbara, and I was frozen.

"You think it's funny, do you?"

"No, no!" Connie was desperate. "*Barb!*" She turned back to face the big blonde desk. "She's just nervous, Mr. Simmons. She doesn't mean it." It sounded like she was talking to John or Monte, soothing somebody my little brothers' size with her voice. Mr. Simmons glared, breathing hard. Finally Barbara's noises stopped, though her chest was still moving in and out. Then, somehow, we were on our way back down the gray and white tiled hallway. My ears rang. It felt as if we were floating.

But as we turned the corner into our classroom I suddenly swallowed the weight of gravity, as if a shovelful of hot stones had tumbled into my stomach. Barbara and Connie had risked all this for me. They didn't know that the real reason I hadn't done the homework assignment wasn't the injustice of being singled out for blame but Mrs. Markle's offhand remark just before the bell rang. "You people don't have anything better to do this evening anyway." How could I explain to them, or to Mrs. Markle herself, for that matter? Poor families aren't good at such explanations. And besides, none of them had seen my mother's eyes.

Round the clock sniper coverage on CNN, the reporters' voices weaving a mat behind our own in Aunt Carolyn's living room. Monte, the youngest of us, had wanted Mom to choose the alternative to the girdlestone: two Total Hip Replacement surgeries, six weeks apart. There would be only a 60-70% chance, with two surgeries, of eliminating the staph infection and saving her life. But she would be able to walk again. Just last fall, though, a specialist had told Mom that the joint cap had already worn through into her pelvis—and that she might not survive replacement surgery anyway. Finally Monte acknowledged her decision to have the girdlestone. "It's best," he said. "I know." He picked up his little boy and wrapped both arms around him.

"Take care. Take care," Mom tells me. She is crying. A day has passed, two days. She has been telling me things that she would not say if she were not reacting to the anesthetic and pain meds. "This is the worst nightmare of my life," she says. "Of my whole life." Is it morphine, or metaphor? "Have fun, be good," our mother had joked as they wheeled her into surgery—the same goodbye that had always made us laugh when we were teenagers. "I'll be okay," she had told me earlier that day. "And if I'm not, that's okay too." But she had lived. She had awakened from this major major surgery. "I have to figure out what to *do*," she says now, jerking awake. We'll get through this, I tell her again. We'll get through it together. "Oh, Bette," she says. Hopeless, this daughter—still. Her eyes close.

Mrs. Markle's husband had worked in the bank, but now he didn't have a job. In the hallway outside the classroom door, we whispered what we had all heard our parents talking about: he had been accused of embezzling money. Mrs. Markle was teaching us how to debate; the rest of the class was still inside, deciding which side had been more convincing. "Resolved: that Algeria should become an independent country." She didn't look different, I thought as we waited—she had the same red cheeks and that gold dress—but she must feel different. As if everyone were staring at her.

John and Monte were feeling better now, back to making their cardboard-box cars with the tuna can headlights and kettle lid steering wheels. After they were well the doctor had told Mom how dangerous their illness had been. It could have been fatal, he said. Why hadn't he told her when they were so sick? Were there things too frightening to say out loud, even if people already knew them without being told? The more I was learning this year, the less I understood.

On the last day of school I waited until I had walked out of the classroom to open my report card. There it was, in turquoise ink. Barbara and Connie and I stood elbow-to-elbow, comparing cards. All three of us had A's in spelling. What about our zero grades on that missing assignment? "She knew what she did was wrong," Barbara said. I didn't say anything. Maybe Mrs. Markle had just decided to forgive us. Bobby and his younger brothers ran by, whooping stair-step images of each other. Their mother had broken the school rules by giving all three boys Mohawk haircuts for the last day of school. "They'll have the whole summer to grow them out," she said as they climbed into her car.

>-⊢◄►-○-◄►⊢-◄

The swing shift crew on the hospital's surgery wing had come in to sing Happy Birthday. Mom would be leaving for Rehab soon, and they wanted to let her know how much she meant to them, this woman who had already turned her wounded leg to the side of the bed, reached for the walker, and stood. The kitchen sent up chocolate cake, and my sister and I had brought one too. Eighty-four. "It's more like she's in her late fifties or early sixties," one CNA told me as the ambulance crew lifted her, laughing, onto the Gurney.

But she is down to nearly 80 pounds now, unable to eat or drink. And even pain medications so strong they make her this nauseated can't take that ghost-pale look from her face. Her white cell count keeps climbing. "I wish I could trade places with you for just an hour or two," I tell her. "Oh God no," she says. They've started an IV drip this morning—glucose, saline, and potassium—but it doesn't seem to be helping. The first week after surgery is the most difficult, the surgeon had told us. It's the end of the second week now—but it feels like we're losing her.

She feels too sick to ride in the wheelchair van to her doctor appointment, and the surgeon sends word that he can't help either; her primary care physician is the one to deal with these problems. But doctors don't come to nursing homes. "She *has* come," my sister insists. "She told Mom that once she sneaked in, in sunglasses and shorts—a disguise so the nursing home staff wouldn't know it was her—but she came!" The Rehab nurses look at their laps. Could we pay for an ambulance to take her, then?

No, the gurney can't get upstairs to the doctor's office. The ambulance can take her only to the Emergency Room. They try to explain: it's unlikely we could find any doctor who will come to the nursing home. Medicare regulations. My brother John repeats what he has said a moment ago: he likes doctors about as well as he likes rattlesnakes. My sister says Mom is lying here looking like a victim of a concentration camp and—

"Call the ambulance," I say.

By the time a doctor has pulled a curtain around the gurney in the crowded Emergency Room hallway and finished his blood tests and X-rays, Mom is beginning to feel better. Maybe the IV just needed time to work. The white count is back down. "Her surgeon says the count will fluctuate, that this is normal," the doctor tells us. "The hip X-ray looks okay." We know how the system works now, I tell John in the parking lot. We'll just have to make it work for Mom. Back at Rehab, the charge nurse—by now she's in tears—tells us that the PIC line is clogged and our mother will have to return to the hospital to have a new one inserted; the antibiotic she's getting every 36 hours is so powerful that it destroys the veins unless they are protected by this plastic tubing. But the procedure goes smoothly and Mom is back in her bed at 10, only four hours behind schedule for the Vancomycin. "I meet such nice people every time I come," she had joked with the hospital staff, who all look familiar by now. She had even shared a cup of microwave popcorn from the nurses' station.

A few days later she is able to endure the transport van ride down the hill to her doctor's office—surface cracks I have never noticed expand to crevasses; the wheelchair is strapped to the floor in the back, behind the bus's rear wheels—and this young woman whose care has made Mom strong enough to survive this surgery explains why it was not possible to come to our mother's bedside. Thirty patients that day, three in intensive care. One of them dying. As always, she holds Mom's hand, talks directly to her, puts test results in her lap so she can see them as they talk. "You were right to go to the Emergency Room if you felt too sick to come in," she says. "Of course it's better if you can come to your appointments here—I know you, know your history—but someone needs to see your face. That's how we know how to help you. You're not just a set of numbers on a blood count."

Jointly: together, in common. In partnership. I feel an ache between my shoulders and something pressing against my chest as the road home winds though the long ravine between Dayton and Pomeroy. I can't step inside my mother's body and direct it to heal. I can't even lie down in the bed and accept her pain for an hour while she walks outside to look at the moon over the river, or to watch the rust-colored leaves blowing up the street. The face I see when I look at the steel hip joint is so much like Mom's that even the nurses get us confused, but it's only a reflection.

"Yes, you can go home for a few days," the doctor had told me this morning. I shouldn't worry; the repeated CT scan was simply an extra precaution because the Rehab staff had called her office so many times to report that Irene's family was extremely upset. "But I want you to be the contact person the next time there are questions. You show so much respect for your mother—you always let her speak for herself." I push my elbow toward the roof of the car, trying hard to stretch my tightened shoulders. We will be able to reach the doctor directly, if another crisis occurs—but my voice isn't the only one. There are five of us. What is the best way to help our mother? Sometimes we have five different ideas.

All the way home I feel the steel joint resting against my thigh, and when I stop for gas I keep my fingers closed around it in my left pocket as the tank fills. I carry it everywhere, even to T'ai Chi class early the next morning. "Let the movement start in the hip," Tom tells us. I try to relax my shoulders. They've caught the sniper, I heard on the way to class. Two snipers: a father and his stepson. A boy.

"You have the bones of a 95-year-old woman," my own doctor told me after my first bone density test. It wasn't for lack of exercise, I know, that my mother's hip joints began to crumble. She had her first hip replacement when she was only a couple of years older than I am now. Weekly Fosamax and daily T'ai Chi and weight-bearing exercise—will it be enough to keep me walking up the trails? "Stork cools wings," I hear our teacher's voice. "Move from the center." My friend Susan isn't in class today; her mother is recovering from surgery too. It's unusual, the doctors said, for a fall to break a shoulder like that: the socket was undamaged, but the ball broke into pieces.

When the others leave I show Tom the small steel ball on its jagged stem. "My sister and brothers couldn't touch it, but I can't seem to let go of it," I tell him. "It's been inside your mother," he says.

That morning, catching up on errands downtown, I stop by to see Traci at Bluehawk Beads, where the baby sleeps behind the counter. "Would you like to hold her?" Traci asks. Her face is glowing. The baby's head tucks against my chest, her small, soft smell covering my cheek. Her eyes are blue like Traci's and my mother's—but it is a tiny version of the T'ai Chi teacher's face that looks up at me. There's a ball in the center of our chest, Tom has told us. A dan t'ien, a circle where chi gathers, then spreads. The place where the two halves of our bodies merge and separate into bilateral symmetry. I hold the baby close. For just a moment I feel her small heart beating against my own.

⤝⊶⊷◯⊶⊷⤝

Thanksgiving: the built-up shoe has arrived and our mother has taken her first steps, bracing herself against the walker. This month will be especially painful, her surgeon says, but she's doing well A textbook case. How long will it take for the scar tissue "joint" to form? Another three months; it will take a full year, though, to heal this wound—there has been such major disturbance of bone, of muscles, ligaments, tendons. *Weapons of mass destruction*, repeat the voices on NPR as I drive home again. *We do not rule out pre-emptive nuclear strikes.* I push the button for silence. A red-tailed hawk waits on a power pole above the sage. How many women in Iraq are returning from visits with their mothers right now? I wonder. How many have a child of their own—a son—and a chant rising in their heads: no, no, no, no? On a rainy corner just above Pataha Creek, a police car hurtles across the double yellow lines, breasting the two cars in his lane—a frenzy of blue and red coming at me head-on. I dive for the narrow shoulder and he slips through.

One morning my son calls. "I don't want you to worry," he says, "when you hear the news. I'm okay." There has been another shooting at the service station where he works. The owner, this time, shot with his own handgun as he confronted intruders. Because he has had a lung removed, the bullet missed his heart—the heart had moved into the empty space—and he is still alive.

Nerve gas spills again at the Umatilla Chemical Weapons Depot, thirty miles downriver from my house. Dropped vials, alarms switched off during the first test burn. The Army assures us again that incinerating the stored chemical weapons, bunkers of rockets loaded with sarin and other nerve agents, will be safe. A young depot security guard three hours into his shift accidentally shoots off his little finger. President Bush orders the troops to be inoculated against smallpox, and says he plans to roll up his own sleeve, too. Next summer there will be enough vaccine for anyone who wants it. We now have a Department of Homeland Security.

By Christmas Mom is reading again and watching "Wives and Daughters" on *Masterpiece Theater*. I stare, gripping the edges of my chair, as she dresses and stands at the sink to comb her hair. "Weight on both legs," they tell her. "Get your balance." Even after it heals, she will be vulnerable to another fall. A big Golden Lab trails the physical therapist like a worried shadow. "His name is R.D.," Deb explains. "For Rescued Dog." After the workout in the therapy room, Mom walks all the way back to her room—Deb pushing the wheelchair close behind her walker. I follow them, reminding myself to breathe.

"Sometimes," Mom tells me afterward, "I feel as if I have no courage at all."

Black ice in the shadows where the road hugs those tall basalt-column cliffs at the edge of the coulee. There's the sign: "Severe Side Wind Ahead." The radio can be spotty here, coming only in bursts along this stretch of road where the FM station fades and I have to switch to AM, but today the voices have kept me loyal company mile after mile. Many front line health care workers, according to *Morning Edition*, are not keen on the idea of smallpox vaccination. In one Connecticut hospital, only three doctors showed up for the inoculation; the nurses' boycott was unanimous. Besides, adds another voice, spending so much of our budget on smallpox prevention means we will not be prepared to respond to other kinds of biological attack.

I am on my way back to Idaho to help my mother move back into her assisted living apartment. We will stop at Aunt Carolyn's house for a celebration lunch, then pack the lightweight wheelchair and walker into the trunk and drive back up the hill. A new bird feeder hangs outside the window above Mom's blue chair, and we have taken down last year's calendar. "I'm back!" she will tell a smiling woman in the Juniper Meadows lobby, reaching for the woman's hand as we wheel her by.

Would she be returning to her apartment if Medicare paid for more than 100 days of nursing home care? The physical therapists are not at all sure she's ready for solo living, even with assistance. I have argued her case in the sisters-and-brothers email that we have all exchanged for the past few weeks. "For me, what it comes down to is her autonomy, her own decision about quality of life as compared to risk." (*You decide, You decide!* the poet Naomi Shihab Nye's children's song playing on the tape deck, and my mother smiling as she listened.) The truth is, I don't believe she would want to stay alive, keep setting down her foot for each painful step, if her hopes of returning home were dashed.

But I may be wrong. These days, I'm not so sure of the answers.

The young sniper is about to be tried in Virginia, a state which executes minors. Laura Bush has postponed her White House poetry symposium so she won't have to accept the Poets Against the War anthology—I had contributed a poem; and mailed a pudgy envelope, too, half a cup of rice in a zippered sandwich bag addressed to Pennsylvania Avenue. "If your enemies are hungry, feed them." Like the radio, I have only words. Feeble connections not strong enough to grow even one broken boy or girl back together.

There have been vigils and marches, though, in dozens of cities. Joint efforts. A million people gathered in London—and as many people crowding the streets of the Capital as had gathered to hear Martin Luther King the summer I was packing for college. Everything, I had thought on that warm August day, was going to change. I could hardly wait. *Deer!* I hit the brakes as a blacktail doe leaps a barbed wire fence and vanishes into the small gully, her body feeling for safety in the land. No others follow; maybe they have stopped, head-high alert in the yellowed grass above the bank.

Now the radio's voices are mourning the loss of seven astronauts. One crewmember was a young woman from a small town in India, we are told; another, an Israeli man whose mother survived the Holocaust. Mike Anderson was an African-American who grew up in Spokane. Did he ever kick through the ankle-deep leaves in that hilltop park near the hospital? Here is a grief we can share, a sorrow we can all agree on. We hear their voices joking with an earthbound guide as they enter the last moments of their mission. No one understands yet, a commentator says into the silence that follows, just why they died. But of course it's a risky business, re-entering the atmosphere at 80,000 miles per hour.

At the foot of the Alpowa grade sun breaks through to light the ancient basalt flows above the Snake River, and I look across the water for the place where the ravine folds over itself like a woman's braided hair. The earth is a teacher, said the Cayuse Indian elders who had come to my classroom to tell us the story of this place. A Klamath woman, one of my students, had helped me understand: we don't count by twos, she said. Odd numbers, threes and fives and sevens, seems more natural to us. The strength comes from the whole, from braiding the outside strands over the center.

It's hard to focus on the highway; I want to lean forward to keep scanning the rimrock. Can the land ever teach us this kind of balance? But balance isn't quite the right word. Living for the whole, living jointly? Maybe non-Natives don't have a place for this kind of wisdom in our language.

Most of the words I have learned this year are words I wish I didn't know. Girdlestone. Daisy cutters.

A pair of Canada geese has crossed the highway to graze in the narrow strip of grass beneath the cliffs—green, even now, in that shelter. How do we get so used to it, I wonder: all those people re-emerging from their metal chrysalis and standing up again in morning sunlight as if the ordinary and the miraculous were inseparable? I glance toward the seat beside me. The small silver ball with its jagged stem is still there. It rolls slightly as the road curves, reflecting the winter sky.

Who Do We Think We Are?

It's hard to imagine, these days: childhood without television. The kids in our class had heard about TV from our *Weekly Readers*, which also promised that soon we'd be able to wear jet packs on our backs and fly above the treetops, but we didn't actually see a television set until a cable stretched up the Clearwater Canyon to Orofino the year we were in fourth grade. At first I was disappointed that Spanky and Alfalfa weren't on the screen every time my friend Barbara clicked the big round dial—*Our Gang* was the first program she had shown me—but Barb just laughed. That wasn't how TV worked. Already the town kids had the schedule memorized: Red Skelton on Tuesday nights, Ed Sullivan on Sundays. Everybody got one station: KLER— "Clear," like the river. Channel 3, Lewiston.

Before long silvery antennas were angling from the roofs and chimneys of our rural neighbors' houses, too. But not from ours. Waste of time, my dad said. The truth was, television was a luxury we couldn't afford.

Finally, the fall I was fourteen, Uncle Everett drove into our driveway and carried a boxy second-hand TV up the porch steps, grinning. How could Dad say no? The two of them went outside and turned a metal aerial while Mom watched the screen and we kids shouted through the window. "She thinks that's better! No, back just a little..." Then Everett drove away, leaving us with a blurry Lloyd Bridges and his underwater bubbles. *Sea Hunt*. We stared until the star spangled banner waved good night and the screen turned completely to snow. Then we blinked, looking at each other for the first time all night. Dad had to be up in only four hours to milk and feed before he drove down the steep mountain grade to his job at the mill, and of course my sister and brothers and I never stayed up this late. Somehow, between nine and midnight, our lives had changed.

There's a TV set in my house now, too. When I am alone I rarely turn it on, but I'm not often alone, and Dean counts down the months between February and August, watching NFL Classics as he waits for the return of the Chicago Bears. He loves old movies, too—Bogart and Lon Chaney, Glenn Ford and John Garfield were the models he studied in the cool, dark theaters of his own childhood, eating popcorn and trying to understand what it might mean, someday, to be a man. Sometimes I yearn for silence. No voices except our own. But at other times it's fun to sit beside him and sink into the shared release of laughter or nostalgia. Together we savor the illusion that the doctors on *ER* are actually in love with each other—in revolving patterns—or, for that matter, that they are actually doctors. Neither of us wants to watch the popular "reality" shows, but according to the ratings we are in the minority here: the dramas most people want to talk about are the Idols, the Survivors, the lucky Bachelors. The person most willing to lie and betray and stick her head into the rat cage for what really matters—the big prize, the money. Which ugly duckling will become a swan? Which one will get a chance to soar above the muddy street before the rich man says, "You're fired!"?

The implications of all this can be frightening. We learn who we are from stories, and television has become our culture's main storyteller. What kinds of stories is it telling us? Well, some of them are purely amazing. Even in the rural West, a long way from Stratford-upon-Avon, we can watch all of Shakespeare's plays on Public Broadcasting. We've seen images of life under the ocean and on Arctic ice floes, pictures from the Kalahari and the rain forest and the moon. We can follow the development of a fetus and watch a baby emerge into the breathing world; we can listen as Bill Moyers asks Margaret Atwood about the chilling approach to childbearing she describes in *The Handmaid's Tale* ("But you don't imagine that could happen here?" he says, and she leans into his question: "Want to bet? Want to lay some bets as to that?").

But it is television itself that makes this kind of programming a rarity. Dozens of commercial channels stream into the homes of cable and satellite subscribers, but just how different are their programs from each other? What messages are we getting? Today's Clear Channel does not refer to a river in Idaho or the small station that gave our family its first glimpse of television—and it reaches over 200 million people, more than 70% of the American public. It's the lifelong literature teacher in me, perhaps, but I worry. If one corporation's coordinated advertising determines the kinds of radio and TV programming and even the live performances so many Americans hear and see, how will they find their way to other ideas, new stories, something that might change their lives? Something that—if they knew about it—they might decide they liked better? Some Clear Channel executives, though, have claimed that any objection to their massive entertainment system reflects an obvious class prejudice. After all, programming based on advertising means that consumers rule; it's all about giving the people what they want. One director, former Republican congressman J.C. Watts, put it this way: "The dogs are eating the dog food." Conservative talk shows, for instance. But "the dogs ain't eating the dog food" offered by liberals, he told *Harper's* essayist Jeff Sharlet, because "you can't force bad dog food on people!" (December 2003).

The dogs are eating the dog food? I feel my own social class hackles rising. "Who do you think you are?" I want to ask this Mr. Watts—a reflex reaction, this expression that would instantly reveal my own working class roots. ("He puts his pants on one leg at a time, doesn't he?" my father used to say.) Far better, I realize as I lay the magazine aside, to wonder who *we* think we are. And why do we think so? What stories is our culture telling us?

And who gets to hear which stories?

Every morning our school bus drove under a railroad trestle, one of those tall wooden structures that span the deep canyons of Idaho. Sometimes we passed through the trestle opening just as a heavy locomotive and car after car of raw pine logs jolted and rattled high above our heads, and we all slid lower in the green vinyl seats, craning our necks for a quick glimpse up through the gigantic beams that leaned against each other like thick black pick-up sticks. The bus passed too quickly to let us understand the engineering, the design of this construction over our heads, and of course we could not share the vista the engineer must have seen from the top. But, like people at the bottom of any social structure looking up, we knew that it took all the pieces working together to keep this weight suspended above us.

I had just started high school when our family got its first TV, and soon I knew as much as my classmates about Dobie Gillis and Sheriff Dillon and Gilligan. But none of us had heard of Richard Wright. *Black Boy* and *Native Son* were not included in our textbooks. We didn't read Wright's story about the man who tunnels his way into a basement and lines his damp walls with dollar bills. What would we have made of it? We had not met Jesse B. Semple, or read Langston Hughes' poem "Let America Be America Again." "It never was America to me," Hughes says in that poem, this "land that never has been yet— / And yet must be—the land where every man is free." In the era of the loyalty oath, these were the wrong stories. When I discovered Ralph Ellison's *Invisible Man*, I was stunned. Is this who we were?

It was massive, an intricately woven darkness that spanned not just a canyon but a continent, yet it was hard to see. From what angle could we focus on such a thing?

"Listen to this," I would tell my own students. "These are the words of William Bradford as he struggles to record how his community tried to build God's City on a Hill—the people he is describing are the Pequot, whose houses the Puritans had surrounded and set on fire:

With the wind all was quickly on a flame, and thereby more were burnt to death than was otherwise slain; It burnt their bowstrings and made them unserviceable; those that 'scaped the fire were slain with the sword, some hewed to pieces, others run through with their rapiers, so as they were quickly dispatched and very few escaped. It was conceived they thus destroyed about 400 at this time. It was a fearful sight to see them thus frying in the fire and the streams of blood quenching the same, and horrible was the stink and scent thereof; but the victory seemed a sweet sacrifice, and they gave the praise thereof to God, who had wrought so wonderfully for them, thus to enclose their enemies in their hands and give them so speedy a victory...

And here is another William, William Apess—one of the few Pequot still alive in 1830, the year of the Indian Removal Act, since most of the survivors of the attack Bradford describes had been sold into slavery generations before—

If black or red skins, or any other skin of color is disgraceful to God, it appears that he has disgraced himself a great deal—for he has made fifteen colored people to one white, and placed them here upon this earth...have you the folly to think that the white man, being one in fifteen or sixteen, are the only beloved images of God? Assemble all nations together in your imagination...suppose these skins were put together, and each skin had its national crimes written upon it—which skin do you think would have the greatest?

Remember what Melville called his whaling ship? Was that another version of the Pequot story? And this! Listen to this first paragraph in a story by a Filipino-American writer named Carlos Bulosan, whose work was popular in the 1940s but somehow silenced in the '50s:

When he first came to this town he had hoped that the silence of other years would not follow him. He had rented a little room near a park where young men and women of many races were always shouting in excited voices over their games. Then, finding that he had no part in their merriment, he moved to another section of the town near a large bakery shop where workers were continuously coming in and out of the building. But even as he stood in the street below his room, they passed by him as though he had not existed at all. So in desperation he moved to another section, in an old but neat rooming house across from the town college. The silence followed him there, had wrapped up his life almost completely, so that now it was five years since he had talked to another human being.

We circled our desks as closely as we could. Was this America? my students and I asked each other. Who have we been? Who do we want to be?

But it is hard to search out stories like these on our own. We don't know where to begin, and we're tired. We've been working all day. If a man drifts across our TV screens in swim flippers, we're going to watch him do it, grateful for the distraction. We tune in to the Super Bowl just to watch the commercials. We're consumers, right? Health care consumers, mental health care consumers, consumers of electricity and education and oil?

Consume: from *con*, with, and *sumere*, to take. To consume, my thumb-worn dictionary tells me, means "to do away with completely, destroy; to spend wastefully, squander; to eat or drink especially in great quantity." None of this would surprise the Pequot people, I suppose. "Did you find everything you need?" the young grocery clerk asks as I hurry back to my cart clutching an armful of yogurt cartons—Yoplait Vanilla Light, my current obsession. He's a member of the Umatilla tribe: I've seen him dancing at the local powwow. "No, more than I need," I answer. He laughs. We should laugh, too, at the video footage of the looter bent nearly to the earth with the weight of that big-screen television set on his back. Or maybe we should cry.

Long before I had heard of television, I learned to question the consumer story. "Poor little Jackie," my mother told me. "All she has is toys." At four, I didn't understand. How could toys be bad? When my older cousins went over to Jackie's house I trailed along, and sure enough, there were all the toys in the world, a room full of toys, like the pictures of Santa's workshop. A giant doll house, two rocking horses, one with stirrups and a real mane; Lincoln logs, games, an easel with finger painting paper and paints on one side and a chalk board on the other, and a rainbow of chalk; stacks of comics, coloring books, a giant watercolor box; a box of sharp new crayons, so many I couldn't count them. Dolls, and more games, and the kind of car you can get in and drive down the sidewalk. A bicycle with training wheels and a giant trike. The toy room was as big as the one-room house we were living in that year, and every spot on the floor was covered. We swarmed over the toys like nesting wasps while Jackie stood alone in the doorway.

Mama was right, I thought when Jackie grew weary of trying to distract us from her toy room and sent us home. Even having a rocking horse isn't everything.

But on the day that I was scuffing my shoes along the sidewalk on the trip back from Jackie's house, only gradually letting go of that magical pony with the real stirrups (I had been too shy and too stricken by Jackie's loneliness to ask if I could sit on it, so I had not actually held that mane and let it fly in the wind as I galloped toward the horizon), a man named George Kennan was the head of the State Department and he too was contemplating the world's toys. "We have about 50% of the world's wealth but only 6.3 % of its population," he would write to his colleagues. "In this situation, we cannot fail to be the object of envy and resentment. Our real task in the coming period is to devise a pattern of relationships which will permit us to maintain this position of disparity without positive detriment to our national security. To do so, we will have to dispense with all sentimentality and daydreaming; and our attention will have to be concentrated everywhere on our immediate national objectives. We need not deceive ourselves that we can afford today the luxury of altruism and world-benefaction... The day is not far off when we are going to have to deal in straight power concepts."

His words chill—mainly because he expresses so bluntly an idea that is in fact a common belief and one that most of us live with quite comfortably. Consumers "rule." It's a railroad bridge sturdy enough to carry all our freight, from Humvees to nuclear waste.

On the morning of September 11, 2001—after I had driven across town to hold my son in my arms just to be sure he was still there, still breathing—I thought, "Now we will have to change. It will be clear, now, that what we are doing doesn't work." My only excuse for such naiveté is that I had grown up in a poor family. We weren't wise in the ways of the world, the politics of oil, Kennan's "straight power concepts." All we knew is that you have to share what you have or things get a lot worse for everybody. If you take all the apples and have to listen to your neighbor's children crying with hunger through the thin walls of your life, you don't get much sleep yourself.

Dog food, indeed.

When our president told us we could begin to heal if we simply returned to our shopping, my heart felt like a stone. But I knew he was looking directly at the beams of that trestle. To maintain our position of disparity in the world, sellers need buyers, and in the "consumers rule" story, everything is for sale.

How can we escape it? TV advertising feeds our human greed, but we had been greedy for a long time before television came along. In fact, almost all of the Native stories I shared in my classroom cautioned against greed, though none offered easy solutions. In the ancient Nez Perce story "The Elk, the Hunter, and His Greedy Father," my students and I quickly recognized the kind of behavior some of us had seen at Little League games, or in our own families. The father belittles his son even though the son is a good hunter, scoffing that *he* had brought in far more game when he was a boy. The young man returns to the hunt. Why does his spirit guide, the Elk, help him kill five herds of elk, far more than his village can use? Then the Elk takes him down into the deep water to show him the slaughtered elk, who are visible now as wounded people. "You have destroyed my people, and now I will leave you," says the spirit elk. The young hunter returns home to die too. And the father—who had been "talking loudly, bragging"—is left to live with his grief.

Killing in anger or killing out of greed, rather than accepting the gift of an animal's sacrifice with thankfulness, is wrong. Taking more than you need means that everyone dies: the animals, and the people whose lives depend on those animals. That much we understood. But there is more to this story. "The young hunter has obligations to his spirit guide," I said to my class, "but he has an equal obligation to obey his father. What do you do when these obligations contradict each other?"

"You cut the meat into smaller pieces," said a young Warm Springs man quietly.

This Nez Perce story, which is more complex than my brief summary of it, follows me like a shadow. I wish I could ask an elder to explain it to me, but I know that is not how stories work. I think the story is intended to remind us that we are connected, all of us, and that ignoring those connections is fatal. I think it means that it matters what story you tell, and what story you listen to.

But education budgets have been slashed—after September 11, we have had other priorities—so this story is no longer taught. Community college students are intelligent, hard-working people, not dogs, but of course most of them will never discover the story of the elk, the hunter, and his greedy father on their own. I despair, but what I feel can't begin to compare with what the Nez Perce, the Nimiipu must have felt when their children were taken away to the boarding schools so they could be taught the right stories. I, not We. Profit, not Dreaming.

Why are we here? How should we live? We hunger for answers, flipping through the channels with our remotes, looking for the story that isn't there. Some of us pound on the doors of the libraries, or the universities. (Can I confess it, now that I am retired? I let anyone sit in on my classes at the community college, whether they had paid their tuition or not.) What stories are they telling at Smith, at Harvard and Princeton? At Stanford? Even the Internet can't reveal the code to unlock those doors. Whose stories are not getting published, and why not? Some of us shoulder our packs and head up into the mountains where we can still see the stars, seeking visions, or we leap from lake to bike to pavement, pounding our way through endless Triathalons, faster and faster, if only...

My mother—who at 88 is still my best teacher in these matters—is more patient. Throughout the difficult hospitalizations of these recent years, the television set in her room was almost never turned on. Once, when pain medications weren't enough, she opened her eyes and asked me to speak the words with her: *I will arise and go now, and go to Innisfree...and I will have some peace there, for peace comes dropping slow / dropping from the veils of the morning to where the cricket sings...for always, night and day, I hear lake water lapping with low sounds by the shore...* The words had first come to her in her high school literature book, the only chance she would ever have to study poetry. She spends her life in a small black wheelchair now, relying on family and caregivers for toileting, bathing, getting dressed. But the traveling library stops by every month, and I mail her books too. "What are you reading?" I ask her nearly every day. She knows it's a code—if she's reading, I know she is still asking, Who are we? Who could we be? That collection of essays by Edward Hoagland is her current favorite, she tells me, and she's re-reading John McPhee. Or, David Sedaris's new book was fun, and yes, she loves *Local Wonders*, Ted Kooser's memoir of seasons and survival. For weeks her answer was the same: *Good Wood*, the collection of essays about people and their relationships to the earth they live on by Oregon State University professor Steve Radosevich. "Don't worry—I'm okay," she finally reassured me. "I'm just savoring this one. I don't want it to end."

Looking for Soapstone

I am afraid of nature
because of nature   I am mortal
—Grace Paley

I knew better. *101 Hikes in the Tillamook Forest* made it sound so easy, though, and I wanted to look for soapstone. I studied the sample of rock on the cabin's kitchen window ledge—a dark gray rectangle, polished on the outside and cut open on one corner to reveal a grain almost like granite, though much finer. Soapstone is soft, almost slippery, someone had told me. Native people made pipe bowls from it, among other things. Slippery? My fingertips explored the cut surface. Compared to basalt, maybe. The best place to find soapstone, according to the hiking guide, was Soapstone Lake. A 2.2 mile round trip, 490 feet of elevation gain, a good family hike for grade school kids. Maybe chunks of soapstone would be lying at the edges of the deep green water, like agates shining just above the wet gravel on an Oregon beach.

Judith Barrington, the friend who had invited me to this cabin on Soapstone Creek, had lost the trail in the meadow when she tried this hike—but today the path through the meadow was clear, the grass trampled as if an army of campers had inhabited the "nice camp site" that the trail guide told me to skirt. Just ford the creek, said the guide, and head on up the hill when the trail gets indistinct. You'll find it again; it's clearly marked on the trees.

Sure enough, I found a narrow trail and a slew of pink ribbons and signs, boundary markers for a timber sale—a disputed sale, the one where a young activist had died last spring when he fell from his platform. Some of the trees bore scars that might have been ancient Forest Service blazes, although I knew they were really just places where windfalls had brushed against the bark. This was a deer trail. But I thought I could poke along up the hill and follow those sale markers back down to the meadow if I didn't find the right way. After all, it was only another half mile to the lake. And, of course, I knew this was a mistake. With my faulty sense of direction I have learned long ago to stay on clearly marked trails, and it was foolish to be hiking alone anyway when nobody knew where I was or would notice if I didn't return. I had been sharing the Soapstone Creek cabin all week with Judith, but her duties had called her back to the city for a few days.

"Are you sure you're okay to stay here alone?" she had asked me. Many people find themselves a bit nervous, she said, even when someone else is there. All those windows, all those trees! I had laughed. Of course I would miss her company, I told her, but I would enjoy the solitude too. After all, I had grown up with coyotes and stars.

So why had I had picked up a walking stick this morning? I never use one—a stick jars my stride, beats a noisy tattoo on the earth. And just what do you think you could fend off with a walking stick, anyway? I had asked myself. But the voice in my head had not been thinking of cougars or bears. A *woman alone, a woman alone.* That warning I have been hearing all my life. And resisting: it's a trap, I protested when I felt it descending around me as a teenager. A socially imposed imprisonment of fear. Yet there I was, gripping a twisted tree branch as if it were a weapon.

Of course I was a woman, I told myself; and true, no one else was with me. What was so frightening about that? But I couldn't get the words out of my head, and each stride away from the shelter of my car—the only car parked at the trailhead—struck the earth to the their cadence. Woman. Alone. I thought about my mother—the human cost of her years on the homestead, miles from other women, from books. From the shared grace of laughter. And my grandmother, who had inherited a life sentence of social isolation with her first intake of newborn breath.

Still, it had been a lovely half mile, forest and fern, the trail smooth and wide, that soft, cushioned earth hikers find on the west side of the Cascades. Blue sky, sun and shade. I had even crossed the creek without getting wet. And here I was, cross-country trekking. You shouldn't go on, I told myself as the deer trail thinned and finally disappeared. Still, the ridge looked so easy, looking back. Enough light through the Douglas firs to color the blanket of wood sorrel, and no brush to block the view. See? Just downhill to the creek if I don't find the real trail.

But the trees seemed to be growing closer together; it was hard to get a feel for what lay beyond them. Maybe I should head back to the meadow. It had been a nice hike even if I hadn't found the lake.

When I turned around, I was not where I thought I was. How could I not be? I found a fading pink ribbon, but it didn't seem to be part of the earlier boundary markers. Could the timber surveyors have followed a section line onto a different ridge? Maybe the land had angled and I hadn't noticed. The same emerald wood sorrel spread across the forest floor but now there were windfalls, too, sinkholes of branches and moss. Nothing looked the way it had when I'd looked back—several times, being careful—to check my bearings on the way up. Finally, though, there it was, the steep deer trail down to the creek. A bit of heart pounding over nothing.

Except that this wasn't the same place where I had crossed the creek. There were high banks on both sides. I stepped quickly through the shallowest places, still trying to keep my shoes dry. No meadow. I must have veered right. I went on downstream, wading now. There. That big log. But when I had splashed and scraped under it, I knew it was the wrong log. Farther on? Nothing looked familiar. Better try back upstream. No—and the creek was getting smaller, a lot smaller. Maybe this wasn't Soapstone Creek at all but one of those little feeder creeks. It would be easy to get even more turned around if I followed the wrong drainage. Sure enough, the guide book's map—about two inches square, I could barely see it with my bifocal contacts—showed another small creek. It joined Soapstone Creek just above the meadow. So I'd head downstream. If this was the feeder creek, I'd find the meadow. If it was Soapstone Creek, I'd hit the highway. Eventually.

I was talking out loud now, directions, encouragement, castigations. How could you be *lost* when you didn't get more than a quarter mile away from the meadow? No matches, no flashlight. I had water—water everywhere—and a few ginger snaps and Wheat Thins, an apple I had been living with since April. Binoculars, camera, sunglasses. The long-sleeved shirt, at least. No cell phone—it probably doesn't work here, I had thought when I arrived at the Soapstone cabin and set it aside. Every now and then I yelled "Hello!" Maybe there really were others out there, parties of competent men and women with compasses and topographic maps. It was July, so I had lots of light, and still early afternoon. I had left a note on the table, but Judith wouldn't find it until Thursday.

Woman Spends Four Nights in Woods One-Half Mile from her Car. Would I still care enough to be embarrassed?

Of course it wasn't really likely that I'd be out here for four days—unless I broke an ankle in the creek or on the windfalls. If these big gray slabs under my feet weren't soapstone they were something just as slippery and the banks were impossible, most places. Stay where you are, goes the standard advice, and wait for someone to find you. But how could I face them, assuming anyone ever came? Take your time, I told myself. Your biggest danger is getting in a hurry. Just last month I had read that you are not actually supposed to follow a creek out. I couldn't remember why, but it was something dire. Yes, and the woman in Molly Gloss's novel *Wild Life* had tried this tactic too, just a few miles northwest of here; maybe I too would see the Sasquatch family soon.

What if this isn't Soapstone Creek? I worried. If the timber sale ribbons had led me onto another slope it might be a creek not even shown on my map. I had guessed wrong by 180 degrees more times than I wanted to remember; I could easily be that disoriented. Any creek in the Tillamook Forest would take me toward the Pacific, of course—but what if the distance was far greater than I could wade in an afternoon? The ocean was, what, twenty miles west as the crow flies? If you don't make it out by dark you'll be cold, but you won't freeze, I kept telling myself. Tracks everywhere—elk, deer, a coyote, raccoon. I might hear them walking past in the night, family members who know their way through the darkest rooms.

Then I saw a dipper. "Lead me home, little dipper," I said. The gray bird bobbed and swam downstream. Another dipper joined her. They kept just ahead of me. I had to wade up to my thighs in some places, hanging on to rocks and branches. Backtracking, climbing out to make wide half-circles through the shadows of the tall cedars and firs when the tangles of windfalls over the creek were impassable. I was an initiate outside the gates of these mysteries, waiting to be let into the earth.

My mother really did see a Sasquatch. It was walking up the bed of the small creek that flowed from the steep Washington side of the Columbia Gorge into the river just below Bonneville Dam. Not far away, thirty or forty feet, and though the legs were hidden behind the creekside berm she could see the upper body clearly through the morning mist. "It was pretty special," she told me, her voice quiet. To recognize earth's mysteries, we have to be receptive to them.

But I had to focus ahead, looking for footholds that wouldn't betray me. Tonight there would be bats dipping above these waters—last week Judith and I had sat at the edge of the creek in front of the cabin at dusk as bats arced so swiftly toward the paling current that my human eyes could catch only a flicker of motion dissolving again to darkness. Beauty too swift for thought: is that why people are afraid of them? Or is this simply another fear we have been taught? Night birds would be hunting here too. Owls. "If you find one of these on the road, don't bring it to me," a Umatilla tribal elder once told our bird club. And just as his slide of a Great Horned Owl had illuminated the front row of faces in the damp church basement, a small bat had emerged from some sheltered corner and clung to the bright screen as if kissing those gray-white feathers for solace. Then it was off again, wing-bones bumping the low ceiling. The owl had stared silence as birders ducked in their folding chairs. A woman behind me covered her face. "Evil is all right if you know how to deal with it," Louie Dick was saying, unaware of the distraction. "But I don't." Breathless—an effect of his diabetes—he lowered himself into his own folding chair just as a tall woman stood, waving her coat. "Besides," he said, "there's a way to gather birds. Oh, a bat! Good." He smiled, then turned back to the slide: he had something more to tell us. The woman lunged for the bat.

His words had settled over my shoulders like a jacket of shadows. Once, long ago, an owl "like a sorrel horse" (and I saw it, a vivid image, though I had never imagined such an owl) had plummeted from a blazing August sky to strike his small-boy shoulder, swooping at him again and then a third time. At last he drove it away with a fistful of dusty stones. Safely home, his hair still damp from the morning's play in the river as he sat down to lunch, he told his grandmother what had happened. She burst into sobs. A few days later, he lost someone he loved.

Behind me people had begun to sit upright. "Eagle is the bird of sun," he was saying. "Owl is the bird of the moon."

Something pink up ahead now. Another sign—the timber sale again? But this one was bigger. I had to ford the creek, back and forth around a big log jam, and then splash back upstream to read it. SALMON SPAWNING CREEK. On the bottom of the sign, in fading permanent-marker letters, someone had written "Soapstone Creek" and some coded numbers. I wanted to embrace whoever it was and shout. And someone had walked out on this logjam to staple the sign. I scanned the steep banks, but there was no sign of a trail. Had I come far enough that I was already close to the highway? Maybe this person had simply walked down over the hill. I listened hard, but I could hear only the dippers.

Do the people who find their way through the world without wading down creek beds simply know the right stories, I wondered? The ones that will keep them from getting lost? Perhaps confidence emanates from the very fabric of their high-tech hiking gear—North Face jackets layered over Capilene, boots lined with Gore-Tex. Or maybe these hikers' minds are simply not so busy reminding them of their self-doubts. This week at the cabin I had been reading a book that had me thinking hard about fear and how it might be possible for anyone to walk through the world without it. Feeling fear, Calvin Luther Martin had been telling me in *The Way of the Human Being*, actually creates a fearsome universe—especially that fear of the natural world, of the "wild," the "other," that most Western European cultures seem to share. Meeting the world with compassion, trust, and courtesy in our relationships with others—others including snakes, spiders, and grizzlys—creates a different reality, the reality of both the Navajo and Yupiit who had shared their ideas with him, and in fact the reality of most

Native peoples of this continent. He reminded me of the paradox inherent in quantum mechanics, that wave-and-particle business that physicists call superposition. Humans participate in creating every event: what we look for, our instrument of measurement, affects what we find. Will we measure the world in fear or trust?

It had been easy enough to agree with Martin's ideas as I lay in bed with the windows open to the sound of the creek below the sleeping loft. The natural world has always seemed more reassuring than threatening, and Martin was speaking to something I have been pursuing for a long time, truths I recognized as a child and have never quite been able to deny. If superposition means that events are somehow at their root non-localized, what kind of kinship—between animals and humans, say, or across what we have learned to call time—would be impossible? Couldn't a bear offer his body to feed yours? Or an elk, or a deer? A salmon? Indian women near my home call the roots they dig every spring "little sisters," and there are stories about huckleberries keeping watch on us through their blossom-end eyes. So of course, I thought now, a bird could warn you that someone you love is about to die. And a pair of dippers can guide you back to the trail of your own life.

But that owl in Louie Dick's story had been more than a warning. *Evil is all right if you know how to deal with it,* he had said. "Is the moon evil, then?" I had asked him after the bird club meeting. "Oh no," he told me. "A star. Just a large star." When you ask the wrong question, of course, you can't hope to understand the answer. My foot slid around a wet boulder, jamming my leg against a jagged snag. But the walking stick held, and the raw scrape was already numbing in this cold water. I felt a quick ripple of memory, like a wing-brush of air against my cheek: once, a Great Horned Owl had swooped over me in pre-dawn darkness. I had been lying on the slope above the old millpond near the foxes' den, watching the last pale streaks of the summer meteor shower. What a gift! I thought as my eyes made out that looming shape. And then it came again. It had taken me a few minutes to realize that the owl, whose killing strike is as powerful as the bald eagle's, had been checking to see if I were prey.

But Louie Dick's grandmother had not been afraid of the natural world itself. Bird of the moon. The waning moon, sliding from its full circle of light toward that sharp, thin scimitar that hangs white as bone in the morning sky and finally disappears completely? She feared the death she knew was coming. The anguish of loss, of human grief. And anguish can be magnified to unbearable proportions if it is caused by the kind of destructive malevolence that it takes a powerful medicine person to balance, or—no,

I had circled back to my own fears. My own definition of evil. Those exclusions I had been struggling against all my life, classifications and separations into Otherness that ultimately lead to bayonet charges and death camps. Deliberate human cruelty—is there anything, really, more terrifying? But I was pretty sure Louie Dick had meant something else.

Besides, my mind was taking me pretty far away from rivers and birds and moons. What truths could I have learned from my own grandmother, I wondered—Emily, the woman I would be born too late to meet?

Just ahead, a stand of vine maples arched over a green pool. The current here, whatever force led to those riffles beyond the gravel bar, was barely visible. I remembered the sudden holes in the Clearwater, that Idaho river of my childhood, and how it feels when your wet hand slips from the inner tube that has carried you through whitewater riffles just above glistening river rock and a chilled darkness opens beneath your feet. Where has it come from, this cavern that spreads its jaws to swallow what had been a clear-flowing path, a road you thought you knew how to measure? You pull yourself back to the surface, your arms flailing.

But of course a person can't do that in January, when the icy shock of the fall has left her paralyzed. What had called Emily down from that narrow bridge? In the black and white photographs I had scanned so carefully for clues, she was only a small, dark-haired woman trying to smile directly into the sun. Did she really believe the voices that told her, again and again, that she didn't belong anywhere on this earth? *Illegitimate, impoverished, female. Melancholic.*

It's easy to fall prey to such voices, I know. You can be trapped inside their fences even when you think you're rebelling against them, out there manning the barricades. Not good enough, not smart enough, don't have the password. Can't walk through the world. Can't make it home.

But this was a creek, not a river; the pool was only waist deep. About four more miles, I guessed, squinting again at the little map. Just be careful. A slow half-mile later, I heard something. A jet, probably. No—a log truck, climbing a grade. Compression on the down slope, then up again. Where? The sound seemed to come in a half circle, almost 180 degrees. Did I dare crash my way through the deadfalls up the hill? I was loath to leave the creek and those printed words. But I found a clear chute up the steep ravine—double-checking as I climbed to make sure I could look back down and not lose sight of the water—and waited. If that was the road above me, I ought to be able to hear regular traffic. And finally, there it was. An SUV, probably. Or a pickup. Close, maybe 75 yards, just over the ridge. Sure enough—so near, after all, just beyond that patch of fireweed—I recognized the asphalt rim of a highway.

Lost Woman was suddenly an ordinary hiker, resolute and strangely soggy, with a day pack and walking stick—not much shoulder, four wheel drive crew-cabs zipping so close to the white line that I could feel their breath. I passed mile marker 5, and there was the Forest Service side road to the trailhead. Moving with such little effort felt almost like running—or rather, those dreams of running, when my feet barely touch down and the earth feels like sky. Was it possible that my legs could be this light? On a surface like this I could walk forever, I could walk to the ocean. But more than that. Something else. I had lost the marked human trail and another pattern had opened ahead of me; not the easiest or safest or quickest way back to my car, but a way as natural as gravity. At the top of the long hill I saw my car—a green so dark it can look black. In the sunlight it was the color of underwater, glittery moss.

I laid the walking stick in the trunk. It was just a tree branch, but it still felt like a cousin—like the dipper, like the Fish and Wildlife worker who was trying to undo our human damage to the world. I was kin to the log truck driver, too, I thought—the man or woman who would soon be hauling those trees from a clear cut where pink ribbons rotted in oily sawdust. And the stockholders of the lumber companies in their big houses overlooking the ocean? Them too? When my key turned in the ignition there was Terry Gross, telling me all about Ira Gershwin and Rosemary Clooney as if the world were the same as it has always been. Out on the highway I turned right instead of left and wound down the grade to the seedy-looking crossroads market. When my eyes had adjusted to the dimness I squeezed past the *Hustler* magazine rack to buy a diet Pepsi and a huge cup of ice. Maybe the guy behind the counter volunteers with the sheriff's posse to help find lost hikers.

The last light had left the mountain when, already warmed by a bowl of stew, I climbed into the Jacuzzi on the cabin's back porch and sank into steaming water. I had carried a tape player outside, Naomi Shihab Nye's voice turned up loud enough to hear over the pulsing jets. Only a couple of bruises. "You make a simple pact with the simple facts, and you'll find you don't need much more," Naomi sang. I remembered a Native man telling me, a long time ago in another forest, "Look down. You are walking on medicine."

Would that medicine have felt this soft under my shoulder if I'd had to sleep beside the creek? I made a human-sized nest under the loft bed's thick green comforter, and located the big dipper through the skylight. The closest spruce was a massive shape leaning toward the corner of the cabin. I almost said it aloud: *Shelter in place.* But of course the words of this slogan repeated so often in my local news do not refer to the comfort I had found in the "this way!" call of the dipper or the soap-and-shower trappings of Judith's cabin. "Shelter in place" is the public safety officials' way of reminding us to keep a ready supply of plastic and duct tape and AA batteries on hand in case of a major nerve gas leak as army contractors incinerate the sarin and mustard gas and GB rockets stockpiled in eastern Oregon—just off the freeway—during the Cold War

"Fear, let me be emphatic, works," Martin had written. "It is genuine, and it is reasonable and logical and coherent and flawless: but only within its own reality."

My grandmother left so few stories in her Big Chief tablet, and the round pencil script is fading. In her stories, everyone belongs in this world and borders are permeable. "Before you know what kindness really is / you must lose things," says one of my favorite Naomi Nye poems. "You must travel where the Indian in a white poncho / lies dead by the side of the road. You must see how this could be you..." My legs remembered the push of current, like a shadow against the back of my thighs, and I could feel my feet still reaching for those teetering points of balance. When I opened my eyes again the stars had drifted into a new pattern in the skylight. Beneath the open window, water from Soapstone Lake was falling toward the Pacific.

Considering the Possibilities

Some life lessons become clear even as I'm learning them, lost and wading waist-deep down a creek. But most take me much longer. It's in the very definition, I console myself: life lessons. "Time is but the stream I go a-fishing in," wrote Thoreau, and I still see whole schools of fish in that green current, flickering shadows of questions my mind keeps darting after like an ever-hungry minnow. For instance: if I have come to believe I am a worthy human being who belongs in the Blue Sky Restaurant, or the fabric shop—or anywhere I want to walk—does that mean there are others who do not? If everyone belongs, why use that word at all? And what is a "worthy human being"? Worth what? Who decides? Already I'm tumbling in whitewater, topsy-turvy, gasping for air. "Once someone goes off to college," Franny had asked me, "doesn't everything change?" It was Jan who had answered, speaking when I couldn't: "Somehow, you never quite leave it behind you." I remember feeling grateful that someone understood. Yet hadn't I been determined to help change things, as desperate to learn the stories and to pass them on as if I thought they could close every wound? Every life torn open by the violence inherent in "otherness"—the separations by race and gender, or social class, by that which we think we understand, that which we fear—all those classifications into the worthy and unworthy?

And then there's the big question, the quick shadow I suppose everyone chases into the cold depths sooner or later. What has my life meant? Have all those years in public school classrooms meant anything at all? *The failure of American education*, say the voices coming from my radio, the phrase offered as casually as a weather report, *partly cloudy and cooler*: it's a given, an accepted fact. Merit pay for *good* teachers, someone suggests, might be the answer.

Money. There it is again, coming at us from above, out of the sun from yet another angle. What teacher doesn't need more? Why do I feel this darkness pushing against my chest?

When I started teaching high school in White Swan, Washington, in 1967, I knew I wouldn't have a lot of money. It hadn't occurred to me to choose a career by what it paid—teachers didn't earn much, but that was familiar, a life I knew. It felt awkward, in fact, to be making $5600, a bit more than my hard-working father even though this was my first real job. What did come as a surprise was the discovery that the word "union" wasn't welcomed in the teachers' room. During the Right to Work controversy at the lumber-planing mill, Dad had worn not one but two union buttons pinned to his hat—"Believe me," he said when the younger men complained about paying their dues, "things are a hell of a lot better than they used to be"—but I wasn't trying to make a statement when I called the N.E.A. a union. I just thought that's what it was. No, an older teacher corrected me: the National Educational Association was a professional organization.

In the evenings after those first long days in the classroom, as I sat propped against the wall of my empty living room to eat a bowlful of that week's stew or chili, I wondered how other teachers managed to stretch their budgets enough to buy a kitchen table and chairs, not to mention the shirts and ties this professional role demanded. Here I was cross-legged on the floor, and the only clothes hanging in my closet were the skirts and dresses my mother had sewn for me when I was in college or still in high school myself. I was at the bottom of the salary scale as a beginner, but cash was in short supply even for some of the more experienced teachers. That summer, everyone who was not paying for the summer school sessions required to maintain a teaching certificate found a manual labor job. The shop teacher offered to let me squeeze into the station wagon with the rest of his family before sunrise—the cherry harvest was on, he said. Of course the migrant workers could do this work much more professionally than we could, and we were paid by the amount of fruit we picked. "I wouldn't actually do this myself," said an apricot orchardist's son one hot July afternoon as he punched my ticket and added my two boxes to his cart. "I can't believe how little people get for such hard work."

After I had left my first classroom to earn a master's degree in my subject area, I accepted another position, this time teaching seventh grade English through a long winter in the Flathead Valley of western Montana. I had to chain up my battered Ford Falcon nearly every night for the drive home to an old farmhouse perched on the lap of the Mission Mountains, a beautiful if dangerous journey. "The view is part of your salary," said the principal. Dean and I learned to stretch a chicken for a whole week. I was the only woman in the middle school—and the only teacher who did not have another eight-hour shift to work after classes, pulling on the green chain at the sawmill or pruning and smudging in the local orchards. The men knotted their ties every morning with hardened hands.

Salaries were better in both of the northeastern Oregon high schools where I taught for the next fifteen years—modest enough that I once qualified for food stamp assistance during a difficult few weeks, but better. There were step increases and cost of living adjustments, and even though they did not keep up with the rampant inflation of those decades, they helped. Sometimes the mill workers made more than we did, a fact they liked to kid us about, but we just grinned and elected them to the school board. They knew what life was like for us, and we understood them too. By the time I began teaching at the community college at the foot of the Blue Mountains, I was not surprised to learn that my English Department colleagues had once set chokers in the logging camps, or gutted salmon at the cannery, sorted asparagus on conveyor belts, washed dishes in a café. Nearly all the teachers I had ever met had grown up in working class families; many of us had become teachers at least partly because this was a job we knew about. Teachers had been part of our lives since grade school—unlike cello players and aeronautic engineers, say, or museum curators, who did not live or work in our neighborhoods.

Of course we had to fight for tax levies, and my own painful experience had taught me that we were all subject to losing our jobs at any time if the levies failed, no matter how much praise we had earned on our performance evaluations. But the people of this region were proud of their college and grateful for the opportunities it gave them, so the levies passed. Retirees or men and women out of work or kids who had just graduated from the local high schools could study everything from nursing to philosophy, French and German and classical Greek drama. You could learn to scuba dive or kayak, you could learn to write. Computers, mathematics, history and psychology, civic engineering. The business and agriculture departments were especially popular in the spring when they sold the best bedding plants in town, and when poets came to my classroom I always took them out to watch the Great Pyrenees guarding their sheep. By this time I had reached the middle of the salary scale; I had that kitchen table and some chairs and I could make payments on another house of my own. Were we professionals? I still wasn't sure—teachers seemed to live in a separate section of the city. Kara might be asked to show slides of her spring break biology field trip to Death Valley at a Rotary luncheon, and Don, who taught political science, was a frequent speaker. But only college administrators were invited to be members. And despite the fact that a Wal-Mart Super Store had moved to town and union membership was declining all across the country, everyone agreed that we belonged to one. The National Education Association was indeed a union.

When Oregon joined California's property tax limitation movement, we knew it was not our local community members who had voted yes. Budgets tightened while we waited for our state legislature to find another way to keep funding public schools, but we juggled our schedules and somehow most of our college classes went on—Shakespeare and geology, botany and sociology and Introduction to Poetry. The deans were excited now about something they called Distance Education and wanted us to get in on the ground floor—marketing, they called it. One of them suggested that I should teach Native Literature by electronic correspondence. Don't worry, she said. Your students will be able to chitty-chat online. I thought about the circle of people in my Native Lit. classroom, their laughter and tears, Annie's comfortable silences. Willie, after class: "I was going to tell you guys a story that might help answer some of your questions. Then I decided not to. I can't; the story is too important to me."

But communicating with administrators had never been easy. So I didn't realize that we were in serious trouble until the faculty and staff met one early September morning to welcome our new college president. A petite woman in tall heels, she needed a bit of help to maneuver the wheeled dolly stacked to its full height with budget documents. We were all too familiar with those endless columns of numbers—everyone dreaded the mind-numbing meetings where we stared at them projected on a white screen, proof that we couldn't have the classes or equipment we wanted. The budget reserved a healthy cash carryover, and though we argued about how large it should be, everyone knew that cash reserves were necessary to keep the college stable. "Let's start by tossing out these old ideas," the woman said, and began flinging handfuls of loose pages into her audience. People around me were laughing as sheets of paper fluttered into the laps of the administrators—seated, as always, in the front row—and who could blame them? We were sick of struggling with shrinking resources. But something inside me went on alert. I could hardly breathe. *What's wrong here?* This new president was talking about teaching and learning—words close to my heart—but she was tossing these words into a salad of language more appropriate in a corporate boardroom: education as our product, students as our customers. We could grow our customer base, she said, by expanding into our neighboring communities, so people could get all the courses they needed to complete a degree in five widely spaced locations. But how can we do that by throwing away our budget? I wondered. Won't we have to hire more teachers, more staff? Nursing instructors, writers, historians, scientists? What about buildings, infrastructure? When we broke for lunch I slipped off to the library to find the business articles she had been quoting.

It would take more than a lunch hour to understand. The corporate world was unhappy with us, I learned as the year went on—with public educators in general, and particularly with the college teacher, that elitist know-it-all. The insufferable "sage on the stage" rather than the "guide on the side" they needed for industry's work force training. What we want from you, they were saying, is not critical thinking or a deep liberal arts awareness of how the world works but just-in-time learning, the no-inventory model they had picked up from Japanese car makers—"Hand out the data, the information students need to get a particular job or do a particular task on the job they already have, and get out of the way." We needed to understand that education is a product and students are simply the customers who purchase it as they become just-in-time workers, hired for particular projects and changing career tracks several times in their working lives. Computerized distance education—"alternate modes of delivery"—was the best way to offer such training quickly. And what an opportunity for private enterprise—Education Maintenance Organizations. Who doesn't need to learn? Teachers in their brick and mortar classrooms, according to a report by the Coopers & Lybrand consulting firm, actually represented "significant barriers" to education.

Money, again—money at the top, whipped cream on the education sundae. We are in for a wild ride, I thought, on this union train.

By 2004 Secretary of Education Ron Paige would be calling the National Education Association a terrorist organization. His remark brought an outcry, but from one perspective—the one that fuels the intensifying attack on public education—Paige was absolutely right. What if public education should actually succeed? The truth is, teachers—good teachers—want everyone to have a chance to learn everything. Imagine for a moment a world where everyone had an equal chance to learn everything. Scary stuff.

Union. From unus, one. And -ion, together. Every one. Everything. Given enough resources—money coming from the bottom up—teachers just might be able to eliminate the notion of social class altogether.

>-<>-O-<>-<

"Consider the Possibilities." When my son was small we watched a children's television program with this title. See an idea from this angle, or from this one—the show's fast pace and exuberant young narrators carried Josh and me, fascinated, from image to image. What if there is another way to see the world? I asked the students in my literature classes. Not just another idea you can explain with your own worldview but a completely different way of seeing reality? Could you let yourself drop into it, if only briefly, open your eyes for a quick glimpse? What if Leslie Silko is right: that time is not a line but a sphere, like stepping into a lake where the drops of present and past and future touch you all at once, inseparable from each other? What if everything—everything!—is interconnected? How do you know if you have learned something? Our course goal, I told them, will not be to collect three credits or a letter grade which you can convert to a number (yes, yes, you'll get those) but to be changed, to become a more complete version of yourself. To be more fully human.

Our questions were endless, and none of us were sure of the answers. Why did William Bradford call North America a "hideous and desolate wilderness"? What is "wilderness"? What does it say about us, that we think we know what that word means? How else could human cultures see trees and rivers and prairie grasses?

Your purpose, an administrator had told me when I first started teaching, is to make your students useful and productive members of society. Useful to whom? I had asked.

Most of the community college students came to us in order to qualify for better jobs, and they would. But for me the connection between social class and education was not about jobs; in fact, focusing on education as a means to a paycheck almost always meant limiting the possibilities for my students. I wanted them to have a chance to learn, not just to earn. Look! I said. Here's Baldwin, here's Arthur Miller, here's Simon Ortiz. Listen to this poem by Rosemary Catacalos. See what N. Scott Momaday is doing: three voices on the same page, three angles of vision. Three languages. Let's try it ourselves...

Carla was just finishing a two year nursing program when she stumbled somehow into the Native Lit. course a week after the term started. "This is what I wanted college to be like!" she said after class the first day. "Are there any other classes like this?" An hour later she was enrolled in American Lit. as well. No matter what book I took to class, she asked to borrow it to take home, to finish, to share with her terminally ill husband.

When she traveled to Portland to take her state nursing exams, grieving about having to miss two class sessions, she took my library copy of Toni Morrison's *The Bluest Eye* with her. The next week an e-mail message from the registrar informed me that Carla had withdrawn from school. It's her husband, I thought. But when I finally gathered my courage and called her, the news was better than I had expected. She had passed her nursing exams and her local hospital had offered her immediate work, twelve-hour shifts. That and the one hundred mile commute to the college hadn't allowed her to return the book yet. But she loved it, she said. Couldn't wait to read *Beloved*.

She had added to the English Department dropout statistics, and there would be no humanities credits on her transcript. By every objective measure of accountability both Carla and I had failed; I was even willing to bet the college would have to replace that library book. I hung up the phone feeling jubilant. Tough times lay ahead for her, and nursing is hard work. But Carla would continue to grow, a compassionate, questioning human being.

What teacher doesn't know this feeling? Such moments—or rather, the belief that such moments can happen—is what teaching is all about. Long ago a colleague had told me a story about his summer job on a highway construction crew. The men were spreading asphalt on a blister-hot day when a motorist waiting behind the flagger's stop sign asked them how in the world they were able to do such work in this 118 degree afternoon. They had looked at each other, astonished. "My God. It's 118 degrees?" They had dropped their rakes on the asphalt and headed home. That's what teaching is like, he said. I knew what he meant: now and then we realize with a shock that it just can't be done. No matter how many possibilities we offer our students, waiting just outside the classroom doors are poverty and violence and abuse, a spouse's alcoholism, sick or troubled children, their own double shifts, all those stories we read in their faces every morning. Yet somehow most of us hang onto our rakes and keep going. Who knows when that next miracle might happen?

I had been working as an English teacher for well over three decades—nearly two of them in high schools if I counted that memorable winter I spent with the seventh graders, and then at the community college in rural eastern Oregon—when the college's Board of Directors hired a 23-year veteran of the 82nd Airborne with two faculty votes of "no confidence" in his recent history to replace the previous president. Spending our cash reserves to grow the college as a business had left us broke and broken in a time of shrinking state funding, and the small but stubborn woman had moved on in mid-year. Together with her interim replacement, the faculty had worked out a way to save at least ten teaching positions, but this man had other ideas. "Get ready to rock and roll," he told us.

I was 57, not even close to thinking about retirement. But the stress of battling the corporate education model had been taking its toll. Teachers were checking into the hospital, there had been heart attacks and episodes of major depression, and people had retired with disabilities—one with Post Traumatic Stress Disorder. Another would commit suicide. Insomnia was sapping my own resilience; the face I saw in the morning mirror looked gray, and for the first time in my life, my blood pressure readings were above normal. When I turned on my office computer the morning after the new president was hired I found an e-mail from a friend who had already left the English Department: GET OUT, GET OUT, GET OUT! Two days later, I submitted my resignation letter.

Dropping that rake was hard. My former colleagues were struggling to remain upright under the slash and burn tactics of this new administration, and grateful as I was to escape the daily battering—I didn't have to drive up that hill every day and walk into those halls where shock and grief hung in the air—I felt terrible. I had abandoned not only my students and my friends but some part of my own inner being: I could get by on my reduced early-retirement income, but how could I get through each day without the gifts that had come from teaching?

Still, I had been smart to leave. Elimination of all or nearly all full time faculty was the goal, the new president announced. Part time teachers were better—"fresher," he said—and readily available even in our sparsely populated region because, due to a missing word in the state statute, adjunct faculty didn't technically have to have master's degrees in their teaching subjects. Or even, in some cases, master's degrees. They were cheap—$1500-2000 for a three-month class, with no insurance benefits—and best of all, he said, he could fire them at will. He demanded that flexibility. How many literature classes will the college continue to offer? The courses I had been teaching, American Literature and Native Literature and Northwest Literature, were missing from this year's course schedule, along with Shakespeare and Film and English Literature. A seven-member English Department was now reduced to two, and there were parallel cuts across campus. Academic and vocational programs suffered equally. Did we really need a full-time history teacher, or auto mechanics? An academic-based criminal justice program whose graduates went on to become sociologists or attorneys or judges? "Boutique courses," he scoffed. Teachers may not discuss controversial matters in the classroom, he said when students wanted to know what in the world was going on. New hires—who these might be I couldn't imagine; in the first few months he had fired nearly half of the faculty who had not already fled into retirement and an almost equal number of support staff—were to report not to orientation but to "boot camp." He hired a career Marine to take over as Provost. Unlike educators, he said, military men could make decisions.

"It's simple," he told the newspaper reporter and the concerned citizens who showed up at board meetings. "What the people of this community need is work force training."

What did he mean, I wondered? Community colleges have always provided a balance of two-year vocational degrees—as well as shorter-term certificate programs—and academic transfer degrees, the first half of a four-year college degree. But he had already eliminated the auto body program and reduced the agriculture staff, and the radio instructor position remained unfilled. Then a six-week forklift driving class sponsored by the Krusteaz plant was touted in the newspaper. Another program taught students how to keep the potato processing machines working around the clock at Lamb-Weston. The money to fund these classes came at last partly from their business sponsors, and the college had already hired a full-time grant writer. Collaboration with the nearby Confederated Tribes of the Umatilla Indian Reservation, who had just opened a hotel and casino, led to short-term training and then to a certificate program, finally to a two-year degree in gaming and hospitality.

People need jobs, of course, though not all of these would be living-wage jobs. But wouldn't the casino workers like to study Native Literature as well? What about educating students to become not just workers but thoughtful citizens, people with richer lives? Didn't we still need a liberal arts education, with teachers and fellow students in a classroom where people can exchange ideas and discover possibilities they hadn't even realized existed? Ours had been such an excellent college, with so many dedicated and inspired instructors… "Those who think they want that sort of thing," a former dean had told us a few years earlier when the college contracted with a commercial distance education company to "deliver" our courses, "can always go to Whitman." Whitman College is an excellent private school not fifty miles up the road from our town. At Whitman, no one mentions Distance Ed. and Nobel prizewinners are invited to read their poetry. The only college west of the Mississippi that costs more, one parent had told me proudly, is Stanford.

That first winter of my retirement I thought a lot about conflict. The new president used the language of the battlefield—"Establishing a beachhead." "Pulling the trigger." And our country was at war again; the men and women from the National Guard unit headquartered on the hill across from the college were under fire. Our students, some of them, or people who had been our students. Already one man, the father of a teenager, had been killed, and a boy from the neighboring town had lost his leg. There would be more: news reports were noting that most of the casualties seemed to be soldiers from poor or rural communities. And the survivors, when they finally came home? When would their war be over?

Our own bombardment wasn't physical, but teachers were witnessing the demolition of everything we had been working to create. How many times had I heard us described as people who spend their lives "in the trenches"? Maybe it had always been a battle—class warfare, that phrase politicians unfurl to stop any discussion of the class warfare they are waging themselves.

I knew what we had been fighting for. But the hard truth was—though the local community college seemed an extreme example—union or no union, all across the country public education was under attack, and our side was losing.

OUT OF REACH, announced the lead story's headline in the Portland *Oregonian*. "Higher Tuition and Jammed Classes Mean the Days of Universal Access to College in Oregon are Gone."

A large color photo showed a Portland Community College Anatomy and Physiology instructor reaching into a goldfish bowl filled with slips of paper. An education lottery: he has only eight openings in his class of 60, and a roomful of hopeful students waiting to get in. A forty-year-old man who wants to be a nurse sits in the front row, arms crossed, waiting. His name won't be called.

Programs eliminated, classes eliminated, no room in the courses that remain. Tuition so high that nearly all students work part or full time and borrow thousands of dollars, sometimes tens of thousands, and take six years or more to finish school. Those are the lucky ones. It is happening not just in Oregon but across the country: half of all college-ready low-income students are unable to attend a university, says the national Advisory Committee on Student Financial Assistance. And one in five cannot attend any college.

"What's emerging is the kind of economically segregated higher education system that national leaders have fought four decades to avoid," continues the newspaper article (Bill Graves, Steven Carter, 9/28/03). Thomas Mortenson, senior scholar at the Pell Institute for the Study of Opportunity in Higher Education, says less than 5% of students whose families earn less than $35,000 will earn a degree by the time they are 24. "The rich are getting richer, and the poor are getting poorer," he says. "And instead of being used to bridge the gaps, the higher education system is now being used to make the gaps wider."

I had quit teaching to protect my health, Dean reminded me. I had to let it go. But it was such a short time ago that I had opened my office door each morning with hope, amazed at my own good fortune. "Community College: Part of the Solution!" read the poster on the bulletin board, and the day it appeared I had felt tears coming to my eyes. I kept remembering students like Richard, who had left an established career in the Navy's nuclear submarine service because he wanted to be a teacher. His politics were as conservative as mine were liberal, and we had spent hours arguing about affirmative action. "Be happy someone got in," I had urged him. "You're in, yourself, right? Through whatever hook or crook? So stick your foot in the door, leave a crack for someone else to get through!"

"But anybody could do it, really. Everybody has an equal chance," Richard repeated. "It all comes back to personal responsibility, doesn't it?"

His hard work earned him an Outstanding Oregon Community College Student award that led to scholarships to Whitman, where he would graduate with honors. He loved the political science department and the bright, eager students who shared his classrooms. Unlike most Whitman students, though, Rich had to commute to campus, a fifty-mile drive from the small, mostly Latino community where his wife struggled with outdated textbooks and inadequate resources to teach 35 first-graders. Her yearly salary was $24,000. Every day he passed the fields where migrant workers bent over onions or asparagus.

One day when he stopped by my office to visit he had said, "I'm still not sure I agree with you about affirmative action. But I'm registering as an Independent now. I think I see what you meant. The students here at the community college are every bit as bright as the ones at Whitman. But they don't *know* it." He paused, frowning. "No, that's not it. They know it, but they don't...they don't have the same sense of possibility as the Whitman kids."

"The Whitman students have seen the possibilities," I said, remembering our endless discussions. *Role models, role models. Has someone in your family done it? Someone in your town? It makes a difference, Richard...*

"Yes," he said. "It's not that community college students couldn't do the same things, it's just that so many of those things don't occur to them, or they can't afford them, they're too busy working to pay for school and the rent and food and heat—I overheard some Whitman students talking about summer break, they're heading to Europe, going down to South America to check things out, *Yes, but I'm going to take the LSATs first, don't really plan to go into law but I just thought it might be a good idea...*"

He shook his head. Then he grinned. I was so proud of him. He wanted to come back and teach here at the community college. The political science teaching position would be eliminated next year, but neither of us knew that yet.

Richard's story was not an isolated example. Community colleges are open to anyone, and students who enter feeling out of place or even frightened usually succeed beyond their imaginings. "Write a story about me," said Jerry just before I retired. He had returned to my classroom after a summer of thinking things over. "Tell them how I've changed." When he was chosen to speak at his graduation ceremony, he told the story himself. He would work as a social worker instead of a truck driver now, but what he spoke of was his real transformation, the internal one.

Would the community college continue to attract award-winning students like Richard, or like Stephanie? She too had earned admission and full scholarships to Whitman, too, graduating with an honors English degree. She was at Oregon State University now, one of ten people picked by the National Science Foundation for international study in microbiology. Soil near deep-sea heat vents is especially fascinating, she had told me. And yes, the English degree really helps. She'd have her Ph.D. soon. So would Mike, a young father of four who was studying math at the University of Washington. He wanted to teach, he said. Pass along some of what he got at the community college. Jessica and Danny with their three little ones would be teachers too, English and history. Pamela, whose children began arriving when she was a teenager herself and who had worked for three decades as a waitress, a motel maid, a potato processing assembly line worker ("no talking!"), was taking Native Women Writers and Psychology of Women this term at Portland State. "I smell a Masters!" her advisor had told her when she examined Pamela's literature-heavy transcript. "Come visit me in Camelot," she wrote.

If any students were named for the Outstanding Community College Student award in the first year of my retirement, I missed the announcement. The official Arts and Culture week went on as scheduled, but no poets were invited to campus. There were no visiting sociologists or historians or biologists or Native speakers, no Holocaust survivors. The workshop on racism—the one a group of teachers from several disciplines had organized for their classes every winter term—didn't happen. Many of the people who used to do those things were gone, and those who remained were simply too harried and dispirited to take on fund-raising for extra projects. They were struggling to keep their classes and their jobs. For many students, they knew, this local community college was the only chance.

Here's the problem, said the new president to the newspaper reporter— the faculty is afraid of change.

I thought of Jessica's face glowing in the afternoon classroom light. I had just come from a meeting where I had been told that what the local business and professional community really wanted from us was to teach our students to make change. Jessica didn't understand my discouragement. "But that's what we're learning," she had said—"how to Make Change!"

The weakness of the Student as Customer / Education as Product model, we had explained over and over again to people imposing this model on us, is that students deserve more than what they come to buy. They deserve discovery, new ideas. Areas of new awareness expanding like fractals, taking them places they'd had no idea they wanted to go. That's our job. Give them what they came for, yes, but more, more. Education isn't just information, a commodity you can package and measure and buy. "Bread *and* Roses," I had joked with my students. "Unlimited extra credit to anyone who can sing all the lyrics by the end of the term!"

Most students understood what we were talking about. Every day they dropped by some teacher's office to ask more questions, to say thank you, thank you, I'd had no idea… But according to my daily paper, the new college president scoffed at all this. Offering students more than they came to buy is silly, possibly elitist. "The culture he inherited seemed almost medieval," the editorial page reports: "a group of scholars coming together unfettered by rules or course requirements to impart their personal wisdom to eager students who desired nothing more than to sit at the master's feet." The modern world, he insists, demands "a much more structured model, with rigid performance standards and measured outcomes" (*East Oregonian* 9/28/03).

Teachers had tried to cross this smoking No Man's Land, offering their Course Information Guidelines, their detailed syllabi and their thoughtful, ongoing assessments of what students are actually learning, what seems to be working and what isn't. But the new president's goal was not students whose lives are being transformed. He wanted useful, productive workers. Useful to whom? He knew that answer too.

At the end of the school year the board of directors submitted their evaluation of the president to the newspaper. An unusual step, but they wanted to emphasize their approval. He was doing exactly what they had hired him to do. "The political problem—or popularity gap—is due in large part to a lack of agreement as to what the 'vision' of the institution is, and what the 'college's guiding principles' actually are," one board member wrote. "Those with a 'Harvard on the hill' model are never going to be content with a president whose vision centers on work force development, regional outreach and strict fiscal conservatism and accountability. It is my understanding that the president was hired as a change agent. He has been very effective in redirecting the college." An accompanying editorial quoted this comment and hastened to agree. "Whoever said that said a mouthful... Developing whole workers who appreciate art, drama, music and literature in addition to their knowledge of their craft is a grand calling for this or any other school."

I put down the paper. "What it's really about, of course, is social class," I had written to this editor. "Access to education. And people in rural communities deserve education. We deserve to have our lives expanded, changed." Now I was holding it in my hand, the answer to the challenge I had posed in my letter. "Did you see the editorial?" Dean asked. I couldn't speak; my voice had become a croaky whisper.

Only a few days earlier, this editor had been critical of mandatory testing in public schools. "The politically expedient solution is to talk about managing public education as a business," he had written, "and introducing the concept of competition." Then, he said, the talk turns to vouchers. And vouchers are just the latest code, like state's rights. Anyone older than 40 remembers what state's rights were all about. No child left behind, he said, really means all children left behind. Especially the poor ones.

Couldn't he see that what has been happening at the community college is part of this education-as-business pattern? Maybe if someone talked to him...

But some part of my mind had already recognized the truth. I was simply throwing up a wall of denial against the initial shock of grief. The message was clear. There are workers—useful, productive workers—and there are "whole workers."

Nurse Carla had found us just in time. What was to become of all the other Carlas? The Pamelas?

⤞❈⊙❈⤝

I still see their faces at the most unexpected moments: I might be washing dishes or pushing the grocery cart or walking out to the mailbox, when there they are, Joseph and Sara and Sam, the students who had quietly chosen their desks on the morning classes began after Sept. 11, 2001. "You are in the right place," I had said into that silence. "Learning *always* helps."

Where does it come from, this passionate belief in possibility? The generation I was born into—the one that headed off to college the fall that President Kennedy was still alive—was going to see the end of poverty and racism and sexism. I remember thinking it might not happen until we were twenty-five, maybe even thirty. And of course we would witness the close of this endless twentieth century cycle of war—even though it was the National Defense Education Act that would allow many of us into the universities to begin our quest.

One winter night after I had left the classroom, I lay awake thinking about my life with stories. What difference had I made? I had touched students' lives in the same ways my own teachers had touched mine, but leaving my career just as society was turning away from those youthful goals had left a bitterness that tasted like defeat. "You're still so idealistic," someone had told me. "If you could learn to settle for what's actually possible, you would probably be more effective at making change happen." What is possible? I wasn't sure any more. On the afternoon of my fiftieth birthday, I remembered, I had stood alone on our small patch of lawn watering the young petunias and taking stock. This is it, I realized. This is as much as a girl who grew up in a poor north-central Idaho family could reasonably have expected: to become a teacher in a small rural community college, living in a two-bedroom cottage. No matter how I had felt heading off to the university in my eighteenth autumn with King's voice echoing in my ears. I was going to learn everything, and then—

Water spraying a thin arc into late April sun. *It's a good life. What I do is important.*

That inner voice: *Not the point.*

"Try not to think about it." Dean was awake now too. He pulled me against his chest, offering the familiar comfort of our two bodies spooned to one. But images flashed through my mind like blurry film credits against a theater curtain—my father's hand reaching for his scarred lunch bucket; my own hand not reaching toward that untouched water glass at the Blue Sky restaurant. The face of a woman in my writing group, shocked that my mother could quote Shakespeare to comfort me when I was afraid. How could I learn to settle for less than full humanity for people of every social class and race and gender? The doubled fists of guns and money were in control just now, but words had not lost their power. I had traded teaching stories for writing them, that's all, I told myself—stories about inclusion and exclusion, the human face in every mirror. I was still working toward the same goal.

Except—what if Kingston was right? And of course she was. "One bomb, one grenade...if only the word had as much power..."

Then something—I can't name it; I only know it can't be bought or sold, or killed—drew one more memory from the well of images. I had almost forgotten that warm September day, a year before Jack Fleming came to town. I had been standing with my mother and our white-haired neighbor Nephi near the vegetable display at the Clearwater County Fair, where the air smelled faintly of carrots, fresh sawdust and straw, watching dust motes drift slowly toward the corrugated metal roof of the exhibit hall. Why was this always the grown-ups' favorite place to visit, when all the action was outside, beyond the cotton candy booth? Only half listening, I realized that Nephi had been telling Mom a story—about a sheepherder, someone he'd known years before, who had been badly injured. Broken bones. Alone, of course, and miles from help. The man crawled on his hands and knees for three days, Nephi was saying, to reach another human being and the doctor who would save his life.

Three days. I had been imagining such a thing—could I possibly? even to—when I felt a hand pressing hard on my shoulder and looked up, startled, into Nephi's gray-blue eyes. "Remember this," he told me.

A quick shiver shook my body, and Dean murmured sleepily against the back of my neck. Outside, a thin line of first light snaked above the Blue Mountains, their dark bulk still not visible though when the sun rose they would be bright with snow. The people who have lived at the foot of these mountains for millennia—in fact, all the Native peoples of the inland Northwest, I had learned while I was teaching—tell their most important stories only in winter. Anthropologists offer quick explanations: if people told stories during the busy gathering seasons, the work wouldn't get done. But I wondered. Maybe this taboo has more to do with winter's immeasurable darkness and the muffled silence of a frozen world, and the circle of firelight playing on children's faces as the community gathers shoulder-to-shoulder against the cold. Whatever journeys we are capable of, whatever our lives might become in the face of that darkness, we learn through stories. The possibilities we imagine, the truths we tell. The words we listen to and remember and pass along.

I pulled the blanket close around my shoulder. It was a cold time, all right, and dark. Exactly the right time for our stories. Imagine it, I thought: people gathering in circles, all of us leaning in to hear the truths of every human life. Sheepherders, nurses, soldiers. Grandmothers. I lay there as the light returned, considering the possibilities.

Reader Discussion Guide

Lessons from the Borderlands is a window into the writer's life lessons, offered to the reader to spark examination and contemplation of the experiences shared in the essays. We hope the discussion questions will provide you with additional insight into the writer's life experience and, in doing so, to yours as well.

Do you agree with the writer that social class is *"the area we simply won't talk about"*? Is thinking about your own class of origin or current social class and the way it influences your interpretation of events something you commonly do? Are you comfortable discussing issues of social class as they relate to you?

"Even race and gender issues seem easier to discuss than the issues of class we are all struggling with on a daily basis, don't they?" the writer asks her students. *"But you can't really talk about one without including the others, the strands are braided so closely that the dyes bleed into each other..."* Has this been true in your own experience? Does it seem to be true in the stories she shares from her own classrooms (in "Borders," "Constellations," "Hope, for the Dry Side," "Who Do We Think We Are?" and "Considering the Possibilities")?

Most of the teachers described in the writer's childhood were not good ones, and Jack Fleming, the one she admires, urges her not to become a teacher. Yet she becomes a lifelong teacher of writing and literature. Why, do you think?

"Only the privileged can afford to eat the way my family did when I was growing up," the writer says on page 38, though she has described her family as not privileged. Is this a contradiction? On the same page, she says she can still feel awkward or embarrassed in social situations involving food, but *"not ashamed. Shame is this weight I feel when, even for a moment, I forget what's important. What I have known since I was a child."*

What is she referring to? How do you reconcile the tension between the growing need for Food Banks and the focus on organic foods and/or "eating out" as a social activity?

≋

Does shame in fact describe what the writer feels after the all-girls' assembly described in "Personal Hygiene"? If not, how would you define her emotion? Why does the P.E. teacher speak to the girls the way she does? Why might Mr. Forester have told the story about his high school classmate?

≋

"Is this what it comes down to? Does the confidence to walk freely under the sun grow out of knowing that you have a place to sleep when night returns?" the writer asks (page 62). Do you ever think about having a place to sleep? Why do you think the writer's grandmother Emily is introduced in the chapter about sleep? How does the story Blondie tells relate to the story the writer tells about Blondie?

≋

"It is hard to talk about money. Lacking it can feel awkward, having it when others don't can feel even more awkward" (page 73). Do you agree? How would you describe your own relationship to money? (Is this something you are comfortable doing?) What does the writer learn from the family for whom she baby-sits?

≋

Why do you think the details of Emily's death are included in "Economics," the chapter about money? How does getting lost ("Looking for Soapstone") help bring the writer to some understanding of that death?

≋

Do you see any connections between class and gender in "Body Mechanics"? Would you argue that any such connections have been all but erased by the feminist movement?

≋

How do race and racial history as well as class issues seem to divide the audience in "Art Appreciation"? Why is the writer especially troubled by the question, "What if I had been a teacher in those days, instead of now?"

≈

Do the clothing issues the writer describes in "Getting Dressed" originate in class issues? Or are they gender issues: *the feeling that my real self was all wrong*? Are they common to both men and women, and to people of every social class? Could you tell similar stories? Would you say that these issues are ongoing for the writer, or has she accepted her own clothing choices? What about you?

≈

Why does looking at the stainless steel ball from her mother's hip replacement prosthetic take the narrator of "Jointly" back to a traumatic moment so long in the past? Near the end of this essay about connections and disconnections, she remembers packing for college as thousands gathered to hear Martin Luther King Jr. speak from the steps of the Lincoln Memorial: *"Everything, I had thought on that warm August day, was going to change. I could hardly wait."* How does she feel now?

≈

How does the writer's mother ("Who Do We Think We Are?") teach her to question the "consumers rule" mentality of the marketplace? Her mother is *still my guide in these matters,"* the writer says. How?

≈

As the final essay—in which she thinks about the value of a life spent as a teacher of stories—comes to an end, the writer remembers a vital story from her childhood, and reminds herself that Northwest Native people tell their important stories only in the darkest months. *"Whatever journeys we are capable of, whatever our lives might become in the face of that darkness, we learn through stories. The possibilities we imagine, the truths we tell. The words we listen to and remember and pass along."* What role do you think stories play in giving meaning to our lives? What are your own lived truths?

About the Author

After a 32-year career as a teacher in Northwest rural public high schools and a community college, Bette Lynch Husted lives with her husband in Pendleton, Oregon where she writes, watches birds, practices T'ai Chi, and tries to keep up with a Boston Terrier. Her first collection of memoir essays, *Above the Clearwater: Living on Stolen Land* (Oregon State University Press 2004) was a finalist for the Oregon Book Award and the WILLA Award in Creative Nonfiction, and her works include the chapbook *After Fire* (Puddinghouse 2002) and *At This Distance: Poems* (Wordcraft of Oregon 2010). Her essays, poems, and short fiction have appeared in *Prairie Schooner, Fourth Genre, Northwest Review* and other journals. She was a Fishtrap Fellow and received a 2007 Oregon Arts Commission Award.

CPSIA information can be obtained at www.ICGtesting.com
Printed in the USA
BVOW032339130212

282790BV00003B/1/P